CELTIC'S SMILER

THE NEILLY MOCHAN STORY

PAUL JOHN DYKES

FALSE 9

First Edition.

Published and Produced in 2015 by False 9 Ltd.
An imprint of Read Publishing Ltd
Home Farm, 44 Evesham Road, Cookhill
Alcester, Warwickshire B49 5LJ
www.false9media.com

ISBN: 9781473328150

CONTENTS

ABOUT THE AUTHOR

Paul John Dykes is the author of *The Quality Street Gang*, which was released in 2013.

He currently lives in Dunfermline with his wife Lynsey.

@PaulDykes

ACKNOWLEDGEMENTS

I feel blessed to have been given the opportunity to work on the story of the late, great Neilly Mochan. If there is a word that could possibly encapsulate the iconic, legendary, pioneering and groundbreaking feats of this magnificent Celtic servant then I have yet to hear it.

I would like to take this opportunity to thank Neilly Junior, who has been a phenomenal and constant source of inspiration and support throughout this journey. My gratitude is also extended to that great Celtic gentleman, John McLauchlan, who introduced me to Neilly at the beginning of 2014. John suggested that I should work on this biography and it has been a great honour and privilege to do so.

Neilly's family members have been an immense source of knowledge and wit and my heartfelt thanks go out to Mrs Mary Mochan, Denis Mochan, John Mochan and John Sludden. A special thank you is reserved for James Butler, who has helped me more than he will ever know during our numerous chats over the last 18 months.

Stephen Sullivan, who edited this book, offered a tremendous amount of honesty and advice. It was an absolute pleasure to work alongside such an astute professional and excellent writer.

Duncan Mattocks is the outrageously talented artist who painted the striking portrait of Neilly for the front cover of this book. More of his sublime work can be viewed at www.duncanmattocks.com.

'The Glory & The Dream' by Pat Woods and Tom Campbell was the first Celtic book I ever read. Pat provided me with a wealth of information

for my biography of Neilly and it was an education to spend time with him and chat about the history of Celtic Football Club.

I owe everything I have and do to Lynsey Joanne Dykes, who is the love and light of my life. Writing a book can be an extremely anti-social endeavour and without the support and understanding of my beautiful wife I would never have achieved my greatest dream.

To my mother and father (The Ginger Legend), who gave me the gift of Celtic.

Thank you also to Luke Massey, Mark Kendrick, Benjamin Read and Dane Camille at M&R Films and to everyone else who has assisted me in telling the story of Celtic's Smiler: Melanie, Jamie, Candice, Chick Cameron, James Henry Thompson, the late John Gerard Kelly, Stevie Cairney, John Price, Campbell Laird, John Langan, John Murray, the late Sean Fallon, David Cattanach, Davie Hay, George Connelly, Ward White, Tony Taylor, Hugh McKellar, Billy Murdoch, Sam Henderson, Bobby Wraith, Charlie Gallagher, Richard Purden, David Potter, Evan Williams, John Gorman, Tommy Callaghan, Pat McCluskey, Billy McNeill, Bobby Lennox, John Taggart, John Hughes, Frank Welsh, Mike Jackson, staff at the Mitchell Library in Glasgow and the National Library of Scotland in Edinburgh, Doctor Ed Fitzsimons, Pete St. John, Rodger Baillie, Archie MacPherson, Stephen Murray, Paul Cuddihy, Gary Fitzpatrick, Ally McRoberts, Stuart Bathgate, John McPherson, Lawrence Connolly, Terry Dick, Jamie Fox, Lou Macari, Tom Grant, the late Joe McBride, Jim Platt, David Elliot, Frank Connor, Andy Lynch, Mike Conroy, Charlie Nicholas, Joe Miller, Davie Provan, Jim Craig, Hoppy Miller, Alex Smith, Peter Rundo, Bernie Slaven,

Peter Grant, Bertie Auld, Graeme Morrison, John Fallon, Joe Craig, Pat Stanton, Stuart Balmer, Stevie Chalmers, Father Brian Gowans, Willie Wallace, Brian McClair, Andy Walker, Billy Stark, Frank McAvennie, Danny Crainie and Kenny Dalglish.

CHAPTER 1:

SEPTEMBER STING

Neilly Mochan, the hero of our story, felt a rush of elation as he entered the pitch. It was his field of dreams; the dear green paradise, like the verdant, emerald shoots of September grass matched by half the hoops on that famous Celtic jersey. The select few chosen to wear that shirt represented not just a football club but a whole community. That club, though inclusive of all, held a special appeal for the disparate, oppressed, disenchanted, rebellious and downtrodden. A young man of just 23 summers, Neilly was already known as 'Smiler', and that affectionate moniker was by no means a misnomer.

With his team trailing by a goal after half an hour's play, this little effervescent centre chased a high and aimless punted clearance and reached it before his shambling adversary. One of the most deceptive strikers in the Scottish game and with a burst of speed that befuddled defenders all over the country, Neilly struck the heavy ball of brown leather first time to the surprise of the near-50,000 Celtic Park crowd, with the equaliser rifled low under the goalkeeper's flailing body. It was the first of many goals scored by Neilly Mochan in the hoops at Celtic Park, an occurrence that was often compared to the effects of a firing carronade cannon. Both were born in the same unspectacular Forth Valley village and both produced ferocious cannonballs with a velocity to strike fear into all who had the misfortune to stand in their path.

A master opportunist, Mochan then regaled the terrace ensemble with a goal of beauty that put his side ahead seven minutes after the break. His lob of sheer finesse served notice to the onlooking international selectors, who could not ignore this deadly marksman on such inspirational form. Mochan was the young striker on every football fan's lips, and not just north of the border. Two goals within the sacrosanctity of his beloved Celtic Park had already been scored, and Mochan's fusillade was to continue later still in this remarkable encounter. And it had to.

The lead was surrendered after an hour but Neilly revelled in defensive frailty and had no scruples in latching on to an error just ten minutes from time before being unceremoniously grounded in his opponent's box. The penalty was awarded; the unselfish Mochan allowed his striking partner to take the kick, and the lead was restored.

Yet his side's defences were breached for a third time and, with just five minutes left to play and his sleeves rolled up for the fight, Mochan was beseeched to deliver once again. He duly obliged, latching on to a late cross by sneaking in behind the subject of his relentless torment to complete a momentous hat-trick. Neilly's now-familiar smiling visage was festooned from ear-to-ear.

Neilly Mochan's bravura performance in the hoops at Celtic Park on Saturday 9th September 1950 was nothing short of breathtaking. The fact that he did it in the unfashionable and provincial blue and white hoops of Greenock Morton is the stuff of legend. Mochan's tale is Odyssean in its scale. His journey as rich as the passage of time itself, he would go on to become a fabled pioneer of the Scottish game, a progenitor of European trailblazing success, and an undisputed patriarch of Celtic Football Club.

A favourite of the Wee Dublin End of Cappielow Park long before becoming a veritable icon of the Celtic Park Jungle, Neilly had inspired newly-promoted Morton to this most unlikely of victories. While the Greenock side won Scottish League Division B the previous season, Celtic had gone through their entire Division A league campaign without suffering a home defeat. The beginning of season 1950-51 had already seen Celtic manoeuvre undefeated throughout their League Cup section and, with victories against Lazio in a friendly and Clyde in the Glasgow Cup also behind them, this was an opening day anomaly for a side who would go on to win the Glasgow, Scottish and St Mungo's Cups. Neilly Mochan's goals and a vintage goalkeeping display from Scottish internationalist Jimmy Cowan had secured Morton their first of ten league victories that would ensure their survival in Scotland's top league. The club's manager, Jim Davies, had already fought off Manchester City for the signatures of his two most lauded players.

Neilly had lined up against five men whom he would eventually join to star in a world-record cup final victory seven years later. But not before a much-mooted move down south had turned sour would he finally pull on that green-and-white jersey he held so dear. With his family roots entwined in Donegal at least 70 years before the formation of the Glasgow side, Neilly had patiently held off for a move to paradise. Transfers to the aforementioned Maine Road side as well as Blackpool, Preston and many others had been knocked back as Mochan declared his preference for a move to a Scottish club. His intentions were clear, yet Celtic did not come calling for another three years.

And fans of this unique East End side should be eternally grateful that Robert Kelly eventually gave the move the green light, as the magical story of Celtic Football Club would have been far less colourful without this unassuming man from the industrial hotbed of Carron. Celtic's alchemical history reads like an elaborate fairytale, and few figures have experienced as many triumphs as Neilly Mochan. As a player, trainer and kit-man, Mochan became an integral figure in many of Celtic's greatest teams. A hero of the 1953 Coronation Cup-winning side, the 1953-54 double-winners and the record-breaking 7-1 team of 1957, Neilly went on to become a trusted lieutenant of Jock Stein after hanging up his shooting boots. Under Stein, he was Celtic's first-team trainer throughout the nine-in-a-row era when the club was feared throughout Europe, winning their most glittering prize in 1967 on an unforgettable afternoon in Lisbon. Neilly's successes continued into the 1970s, when ten men won the league in 1979, and into the '80s, when Celtic captured the 100th Scottish Cup Final in typically cavalier fashion. The following season, he watched from the dugout as Celtic clinched a last-day title win at Love Street, and was again on hand for the club's emphatic League and Scottish Cup double in its centenary year of 1988.

From Jimmy McGrory to Tommy Burns, Mochan served under a procession of vintage Celtic figures. But there is no doubt that his contribution to the club enables him to stand comparison with even the greatest of these. Illustrious ex-Celts from Bobby Lennox and Stevie Chalmers to Kenny Dalglish and Charlie Nicholas rhapsodise about a player who represented Scotland at the 1954 World Cup Finals and who was never short of a one-liner or tongue-in-cheek put-down, hence his nickname. Mochan's smile was infectious, as was the high-pitched laugh he produced when playing pranks on everyone from the ground staff to the Lisbon Lions. That "*Hoo-hoo-hoo!*" echoed around the tradition-steeped corridors of Celtic Park for almost forty years.

From the pinnacle of European success to the depths of 1990s despair and the subsequent Fergus McCann takeover, Neilly Mochan saw it all before his untimely passing in August 1994. With 37 years' service and 50 winners' medals in his kitbag, the Mochan legacy is an indelible part of Celtic folk memory. This is the unrivalled story of the man whom team-mates, reporters, opponents and fans alike affectionately referred to as 'Smiler'.

CHAPTER 2:

THE CARRON CANNONBALL

By a lonely prison wall
I heard a young girl calling,
"Michael they have taken you away
For you stole Trevelyan's corn
So the young might see the morn
Now a prison ship lies waiting in the bay"

Low lie the Fields of Athenry
Where once we watched the small free birds fly
Our love was on the wing, we had dreams and songs to sing
It's so lonely round the Fields of Athenry

'The Fields of Athenry' by Pete St. John

The unimaginable suffering of the starving Irish in the late 1840s began with an epidemic of phytophthora infestans, which spread across potato fields like an unstoppable plague. The late blight served not only to darken the luscious green potato leaves of Ireland's fields, but to cast a dark shadow over the already fractured relations between Ireland and the British government. The latter's policy-makers, spearheaded by Charles Trevelyan, nonchalantly stood back and allowed 'God's will' to prevail. As the potato crop continued to fail and the tubers were repeatedly crippled underground, over a million Irish men, women and children starved to death. Many of these victims were already indubitably poor and the worst-off lived, and died a slow harrowing death, in single-room mud cabins. Meanwhile, the wealthiest nation in the world made no effort to relieve neighbours who had become monumentally dependant on the potato for survival. As corpses rotted like potato crops all over the country, London's *Times* newspaper branded Ireland, "A nation of beggars."

The human migration from Ireland was estimated at two million, and the vast majority of these starving souls shipped out to North America. They did so to survive what many Irish Nationalists believed was nothing short of genocide, with the *in absentia* British Government explicit in its execution. County Donegal was amongst the most impoverished of areas during the Irish potato famine and James and Catherine Mochan joined the mass cadaverous exodus as they fled with their family to Lennoxtown, then of Stirlingshire, to seek out work in the thriving Scottish coal mines. Fast forward 40 years and many Irish immigrants all across Scotland were still struggling to find work to feed their young. This prompted the novel idea of forming a charitable football club in the East End of Glasgow in a valiant effort to maintain dinner tables for those hungry children and unemployed.

By the time James Mochan's great grandson, John, married Sarah Dempsie, the Mochan clan had spread from Lennoxtown and Campsie into Carron, where John found parochial but stable employment in the world-famous ironworks. An empire built from the elixir of iron had been the life's blood of Carron since 1759 and it spawned its huge range of iron wares far and wide. Few then would have argued with Carron Company's motto, '*Esto Perpetua*', meaning '*Be Thou Forever*'. From domestic iron baths to iconic red telephone and post office boxes, Carron was an undisputed hotbed of industrial enterprise for generations of Falkirk inhabitants. But perhaps its most famous product was the Carron Cannonade, used in naval warfare. It wouldn't, though, be the last Carron export to produce fearsome cannonballs.

John Mochan was an imposing figure who stood no more than 5' 9" and weighed in at 18 stones. A strong man with mammoth legs and arms that lent themselves to such manual labour as an iron moulder in the foundry, he made valley gutters by hand with such skill that they ceased production upon his retirement. His father and two brothers, James and Neil, also made a living in the ironworks and a four-by-six-inch molten burn scar on John's upper arm was a constant reminder to his family, who may have spotted it during his evening wash in their home's boil-fast sink, of the daily dangers of such endeavours.

Working with Carron Company also gave the Mochans an opportunity to live in one of the firm's many houses in the locality, and their West Carron residence was a simple kitchen bedsit before 5 Park Crescent in Carron became home for the ever-growing family. As John's youngest son Denis Mochan explained: "We had eight children living with our mum and dad in the same house but that was normal in those days. Every family seemed to have six, seven or eight children and we were no different."

Rose was the eldest having been born in April 1921, followed by Nan (November 1923), 'Sadie' Sarah (October 1925), Neil (6th April 1927), William (April 1929), Mary (September 1931), John (March 1934) and Denis

(December 1935). On Wednesday 6th April 1927, Celtic marked the occasion of Neil's birth by paying a visit to his hometown. Willie Maley's side were systematically thrashed 4-1 in a league match at Brockville. 7,000 spectators looked on as Jimmy McGrory was forced to leave the field of play due to injury and, despite the inspired form of Celtic's goalkeeper John Thompson, Falkirk were inspired to victory by their ex-Celt Patsy Gallacher.

By the age of nine, young Neil, who had been named after his grandfather, was awarded a certificate for perfect attendance by John Farrell, who was the father of future Celtic director James and the headmaster at St Francis' Roman Catholic Primary School in Falkirk. The school's motto, *Virtute Et Industria*, would underpin the values held by Neil throughout his life and career and the disciplined standards he was setting at an early age would prove to be defining characteristics of his entire football life. St. Francis Xavier was himself named co-patron of all foreign missions in 1927, and Mochan would go on to travel on every foreign mission undertaken by Celtic Football Club from 1964 until 1994.

With four young boys in this busy working-class household, football was a hugely enjoyable release from the vapidity of day-to-day life, and the Mochan quartet all showed promise from an early age. With their family steeped in Irish tradition, the attraction of Celtic had suffused them as naturally as anyone whose heritage supersedes such decisions. When an emotional attachment overpowers a geographical one, the connection to such an institution is undeniable and bestows its supporters with an incredible sense of belonging, as Denis Mochan recalled. "On a Saturday my dad would be in the pub and then he would go to the 'Shire (Falkirk-based East Stirlingshire) games. But we were all Celtic fans and that would basically be because we went to the Catholic school and we came from an Irish background. I went through to the matches regularly and it was always our Neilly's dream to play for Celtic. I remember a little later, he had brought a big radiogram into the house and it was about the length of the living room with the lid and cupboards at either side. Neilly would come home with about 24 records at a time and in those days it was the big 78s. We would listen to *Radio Eire* on the radio and then some nights Neilly would put 'The Soldier's Song' on and he would be marching about the living room listening to this record and my dad would be trying to get ready for bed and telling him to get it off."

The first-born of eight, Rose moved to her own house three doors away to start a family and her eldest son, James Butler, was able to enjoy his grandparents' household like it was his own. "I was brought up like their brother," James recalled of the Mochan siblings, "and the house they lived in was a four apartment. My grannie and grandad slept downstairs and there were three rooms upstairs, so I often stayed over. The boys were murder to me sometimes. John was quite a quiet lad but Willie was always crabbit and I remember Neilly used to call him 'Pimple' and he hated that. We had an uncle Willie who had a pimple on his nose and people would call him that, so Neilly latched on to this and called Willie 'Pimple' to wind him up. There was one Saturday night and we were all sitting in the living room when I hit Willie with a rolled up paper to annoy him and I remember he whacked me right across the legs. I was only wee at the time so I started roaring and greeting. It was Neilly, not my grandad, who went for Willie and shouted, 'You clown that you are, you don't hit the wean', and Willie took off. I remember that vividly because auld Johnny, my grandad, just sat there not saying a word and Neilly was already acting like the man of the house. Every one of us looked up to him."

With dark smoke bellowing into grey Carron skies and worldwide political and economic unrest developing with palpable global tremors, it was no wonder that an element of bedevilment would be omnipresent within the Mochan and other working-class households. "Neilly would clap his knees and let out a 'Hoo, hoo, hoo' whenever he found something funny or had wound someone up," explained James Butler. "He was always one for having a laugh and lightening the mood and I guess that is where his nickname 'Smiler' came from. If he was ever going to tell you something that was a wee bit controversial, he would stop and look over each shoulder. He knew that there was just the two of us in the room but he would still look around as if someone was listening in. I remember his brother John had been out somewhere and he got in late at night and had gone to bed as he was working in the morning. Neilly left him sleeping until the early hours and then gave him a shake and said, 'Hey sir, is it not time you were up for your work?' Of course, John jumped out of bed thinking that he'd slept in and he started getting ready and that would set Neilly off. He was always on the wind-up. Everyone who knew Neilly Mochan will tell you that he was a joker and a smiler." Denis also remembers the light-hearted nature of his big brother. "Our Neilly was never dour. His nickname of 'Smiler' was a football thing and we never called him that around the house. When you play football, your team-mates or newspaper reporters often give you nicknames and Neilly's was 'Smiler'. He was the oldest of the boys in our house and we used to call him 'Our Big Yin'."

With Scotland the workshop of the world, many of its young males would carve out their livelihoods in the vibrant but exceedingly tough pits and foundries of their communities. As a constant stream of men queued outside the ironworks to join this gregarious workforce, school-leavers as young as 14 were asked to apply in their own handwriting. So did a young Neil Mochan ever seek to follow in his father's footsteps? "One of the good things about coming from Carron," Denis Mochan explained, "was the big iron furnaces. It was a well-paid job but it could be dangerous and it was hard graft. I used to ask Neilly what he would do if things didn't work out with his football and he always said that he'd go straight to Carron Ironworks and earn a good living there and he wasn't joking either. Fortunately he never had to do that."

World War II was underway by the time that Neil Mochan left the Grammar School in Falkirk's Park Street. Undeniably wrought from Carron's industrial hard lands and with a work ethic inherited from the normalcy of his upbringing, Neil's transition into gainful employment was seamless but short-lived. The manual work offered by the Larbert Laundry Firm proved more than manageable for this strong and sturdy fellow, whose nephew, James Butler, remembers Neil's early foray into the laborious but rewarding world of full-time work. "He left the school and got a job with a local laundry firm. He worked on the vans at first delivering to places like Kilsyth and the Raploch, maybe for a month or two, and then he got moved indoors and worked in the dye department. I remember him telling me that he was out delivering one day in the Raploch and he was always a happy, cheery lad and he was going about his business this day, whistling away, when an old wife came out her house and started giving him dog's abuse. Then he realised that he had been whistling an old Irish rebel song. But doing that was different in those days. That was our family history coming out and there must have still been a big Irish influence, more so from those living in Campsie. He was only about 15 at the time. Our family's roots are very much in Ireland and the surname is pronounced Moe-can. It goes way back in Ireland and there are numerous variations of it from Moughan and Moohan but there is only one Mochan in Ireland's phone book now. Names changed all the time back in those days because so many people were illiterate and so the spelling evolved that way. But there are two Mochans buried in Mountcharles Cemetery in County Donegal and it was in Mountcharles where Thomas Mochan married Mary Brogan back in 1818, six generations ago."

Neilly supplemented his work with the laundry firm by playing with Juvenile side Dunipace Thistle, and it was with the 'Pace that Neil Mochan would make a name for himself locally. Utilising his thunderous left foot, Mochan was played at outside-left and had garnered something of a reputation for having a crackerjack shot by the time Denny-born Billy Steel was left mesmerised by the chubby-faced 17-year-old's performance in an otherwise nondescript Juvenile match at Tygetshaugh in June 1944. Billy was himself playing for Greenock Morton at the time and was so impressed with the performance of the slightly bowed-legged Mochan that he recommended him to Cappielow manager Jim Davies, citing the youngster as, "the best prospect in Scotland". Steel had attracted interest from down south, and a move to a top English club was imminent. But three years before leaving Morton for Derby County in a British record £15,500 transfer, he prompted Davies to line up Mochan as his replacement, going on to pay this tribute to the 5' 9" youngster. "Before I go," he said, "I can put you on to a good thing to fill my place at inside-left. He's playing for Dunipace and you should grab him." Without seeing him play, Davies booked Neil Mochan on a trip to Greenock and signed him for the Ton.

The blue-and-white of Morton may not have been Neilly Mochan's first choice of hoops but they may well have offered an opportunity to eventually make that move to Celtic Park. John Langan was another young hopeful whose trips to Paradise from Greenock as a supporter had left him dreaming of a move to the East End of Glasgow and he became Neilly's only youthful accomplice at Cappielow Park. "In 1944, I was playing inside-right for the Greenock Boys' Guild and there was a challenge match against the Glasgow Diocese at Cappielow Park. After the game there was a journey up to St Mungo's Hall for a cup of tea and some speeches. I say this most modestly but I had been the player of the day and word had got around that I was going to sign for Celtic. We had a return match to play and Jimmy McStay was the manager of Celtic at that time and he sent for me before the game. Mr McStay said, 'I've heard good reports about you son, just go out there and play.' But fate intervened because after about 15 minutes the fella who was playing behind me at right-half got carried off, leaving us with ten men due to there being no substitutes in those days. That left me very much out of position as I had to work in other areas of the park. But to his credit, Mr McStay didn't walk away and he sent for me again at the end of the game and said, 'I couldn't see you at your best today but we'll be keeping an eye on you.' Of course, I was disappointed but after that I was over-aged for the Boys' Guild.

"I then signed for the local junior side, Gourock Juniors, when I was 19, and decided to sign amateur forms because that gave you the freedom to play trial matches for professional clubs if the opportunity arose. I was serving my apprenticeship to be a coppersmith at the old Royal Navy torpedo factory on Greenock Road and I remember coming home this day and my mother said that two men were waiting in the living room as they wanted to talk to me. When I walked in, the manager of Morton, Jim Davies, was sitting there with Johnny Crum. Crum had been transferred from Celtic to Morton and was obviously there to convince me that there was life outside of Celtic. They had all the forms laid out but I refused to sign and so Davies asked me to go up to Cappielow for a couple of nights a week to do some training and I agreed to that. When I arrived at Cappielow Park, Neilly Mochan was there and that was how we became friends."

Morton manager, Jim Davies, had made his name with Morton Juniors and as an outspoken Supporter's Club representative before taking over at Cappielow in 1939. He led the club throughout the war years and built an entertaining side that attracted hordes of autograph-hunters as famous guest players were paraded to help swell the club's home crowds during the war. England internationalists Tommy Lawton and Stanley Matthews were two such doyens of the game to play at a stadium affectionately described by a Morton fan of the time as a "bomb hole" with a "pneumonia-conducive, corrugated iron object which serves as a grandstand." As difficult as wartime football was, John Langan looks back on his time at Morton fondly. "Neilly was the only other boy up at Cappielow, there were no youth academies in those days and so it was just him and me," he said. "Neilly was younger than me and had signed from Dunipace Thistle. This was all going on during the war of course and all the players' contracts were torn up and they were allegedly playing for two pounds a week. I remember Stanley Matthews came to play for Morton one afternoon and he wasn't up there for two pounds a week! The following week, Morton were playing the Rangers and Matthews was out playing for Rangers, so they obviously gave him more cash to play and that was the sort of atmosphere during the war years. Due to the blackout, it was very difficult to get out and train without proper lighting and so Morton would put the lights on in the home dressing room and they had sheet metal workers set up some sheets so that the light from the changing room would beam down on to the shadows of the track in front of the stand. Training at that time was all about running, so Neilly and I would be running a hundred yards and then we would adjourn into the away dressing room and do a bit of skipping to get a sweat up. Then we would return to the Morton dressing room and they would give us a small bottle of lemonade, which was something of a luxury during the war.

"The two Morton trainers were aged men. There was a fella called Jimmy Gourlay and another one called Hughie Howitt. Gourlay had played for the Morton and scored the winning goal against Rangers in the 1922 Scottish Cup final. Big Johnny Divers had left Celtic and was playing with the Morton and he and Jimmy Garth were a couple of comedians as well as very good footballers. They would come out for training and go over to the Wee Dublin End, jump over a small wall and go and hide in the stand. You'd see the bright orange tips of their cigarettes away in the darkness when they were meant to be training. Before we were all due to come back in, they would do a few runs and then head back into the changing room and big Divers would say to Gourlay, 'By God Jimmy, you worked us hard tonight.' And we were sitting there knowing what they had been up to. These were supposed to be two pounds a week players but it turned out to be anything but training. Then big Divers would wind Jimmy Gourlay up about his Cup Final goal and say, 'Hey Jimmy, I was talking to a fella the other night and see that goal you scored? This chap said you handled the ball before you hit it.' Old Gourlay would get all worked up about it and would fully go through all the motions to describe how he trapped the ball and hit it from 35 yards out. Neilly and I would be sitting in the corner killing ourselves at all this. Neilly had a very high sense of humour and you could really bring a smile to his face. I think that's why people at Morton called him Smiler Mochan.

"Old Howitt would then tell this story about the ex-Celtic forward, Tommy McInally. Years before, Howitt had somehow managed to convince him to come out of retirement to play a match for Morton. They had an outside-left playing for the Morton and he had a great left foot and Howitt wanted Tommy McInally to just roll the ball in front of this fella's foot. So Tommy came down on the train and got off at the station just behind Cappielow and, as he was walking down the road with Howitt, asked where the nearest pub was. It was only about 30 yards down the street, so they went for a couple of drinks before they went into the stadium. Tommy had been out of the game and had expanded a fair bit but he went out and scored a hat-trick for Morton that day and Howitt was delighted that he had possessed the foresight to get him back into the game. After the match, Howitt was prodding Tommy's tummy and saying, 'As good as you are, if you put yourself in my hands, you'll be even better.' And McInally responded, 'If I thought that I'd have as much pleasure taking it off as I had putting it on, I'd let you.' Neilly loved the old football tales and found all this hilarious, and this was what constituted training during the war at Cappielow.

"One night, Jim Davies said he wanted to speak to me after training and he told me that he wanted to see me playing in a reserve game. This was obviously another stage of trying to get me to sign for Morton. I agreed to play and so he gave me the fixtures list. We were due to play Celtic at Cappielow in about three weeks' time, so I told him that I'd play against Celtic. Davies hit the book down and said, 'I bloody knew that you would say that. You're hoping to play well and sign for Celtic.' Then he said, 'Right, you're in the team and you have three weeks to get ready.' With about two weeks to go until the game I received my Navy papers and I went down to see Davies and told him that it was neither Morton nor Celtic that I'd be going to as I was off to Chatham. I believe that Neilly did his national service in the RAF, so I lost touch with him for a while."

Langan, like his friend Mochan, had dreamt of pulling on the green and white hoops and had hoped that Morton would be his passport to Celtic Park. The war years and conscription affected John in many ways and by the time he returned from the Navy, his football aspirations had all but diminished. Although his undoubted ability had served him well during his national service, where he spent most of his time in the Far East, his experience of witnessing how the British Empire had treated the natives left him hollow, and he lost his edge for a simple game of football, turning his attentions instead to his trade union upon returning to Scotland. The egalitarian John was lost to the game and became a hugely successful full-time official of the Coppersmith's Union and later a highly respected chairman, and renowned speaker, of the Scottish Trades Union Congress. Neilly Mochan, like his brothers Willie and John after him, was also called up and, despite it hindering his fledgling football career, dutifully complied without a word of complaint. Neilly might just as easily have drifted from the game having endured two years' service as a rear-gunner for the RAF in India. To his credit and the eternal benefit of Celtic Football Club, he reacquainted himself with that heavy ball of brown leather for the beginning of Morton's 1948-49 campaign. It was the season in which Smiler Mochan would finally establish himself as the Greenock club's greatest discovery in years.

CHAPTER 3:

TALES FROM THE WEE DUBLIN END

"I shall always be grateful to John Divers and Jimmy Whyte, who gave me great encouragement and guidance in my early days with Morton. They were a very good side indeed and in fact lost to Rangers 1-0 in the 1948 Scottish Cup final after drawing in the first match. Although I was in the forces at that time I played with the same players on my return to Greenock." - Neilly Mochan.

On 14 June 1948, a dark-haired, 21-year-old soldier weighing in at ten stones and six pounds received his demobilisation papers and returned to Stirlingshire to resume a burgeoning football career. Younger brother Willie, by now rated at least equal to Neilly as a player, was at this time still in the Forces, while 14-year-old John and 12-year-old Denis were showing up well for St. Modan's and St. Francis' schools respectively. Neilly had missed the Scottish Cup final matches against Rangers by two short months, and the combined crowds of just under 263,000 illustrated the spectacular post-war upsurge in interest around the Scottish game. The romanticists, or revisionists, among the Morton crowd at Hampden Park claim that the Rangers winner was assisted by a blinding camera light, which undid Scottish international goalkeeper, Jimmy Cowan, in extra time. The showpiece final appearance, with Celtic having been disposed of in the semi-finals, would have given Mochan some semblance of confidence for the season ahead. Despite the club having cashed in on Jimmy Garth, to Preston; Johnny Kelly, to Barnsley;

John McIness, to Chelsea; and star-spotter Billy Steel, to Derby County, in the two years that Neilly was in Indian skies. Jim Davies had certainly shown talent in identifying home-grown players and finding the correct Greenock blend. But the readiness of the Morton board to do business with alluring English league clubs at every opportunity would ultimately be the team's undoing.

Neil Mochan had played in unofficial wartime league matches as early as 1945 but, after his two-year Indian exile, would not have expected to start for Morton's first team in their opening League Division A encounter at Celtic Park on 14th August 1948. Colin Liddell was struck down by a flu virus, though, and Mochan accepted this unexpected break with alacrity as he made his long-awaited debut at outside-left. Another debutant on the sun-drenched pitch was big-money Celtic left-winger, Charlie Tully, who had recently moved from the club's Belfast namesakes. Little did the 50,070 crowd realise but they were about to enjoy their first glimpse of two players who would prove pivotal in many of the club's finest 1950s successes. During this goalless draw, that prince of goalkeepers, Jimmy Cowan, continually thwarted a Celtic side who were vastly improved from their disastrous previous campaign of near-relegation. Mochan, for his part, caused enough problems in the home side's defence to stake his claim for a regular starting berth as Morton sought to maintain the top division status they had enjoyed since the first official post-war season of 1946-47. Mochan had finally been propelled into the Ton's first eleven and his cherished football journey had fittingly began at the pantheon of Celtic Park.

Although revered as an outside-left, it was at centre-forward that

Mochan shone in Morton's early-season League Cup outings. Drawn in Section D along with Aberdeen, Saint Mirren and Third Lanark, Neilly scored eight goals in six matches and sparked up a potent partnership with Tommy Orr, the Glasgow University student who would be the brains of the Morton attack for his entire 16-year playing career. Orr, along with Jimmy Cowan and wing-half Billy Campbell, were the international-class stars of this impressive Morton side, and cartoon images of them in action adorned the much sought-after and collectable cigarette cards of the time. In fact, Cowan is widely regarded as the greatest Morton player of all time, and Campbell had been chased by Manchester United the previous season, when the Old Trafford side attempted to swap him for ex-Celt Jimmy Delaney. Mochan, therefore, was shining brightly in exceedingly good company.

The 15,000 who attended Cappielow to witness a Mochan double against Third Lanark in Morton's 2-1 League Cup win gave an indication of the growing popularity of the Scottish game during the immediate post-war period. This type of crowd was not unusual and Morton had averaged attendances of 10,000 during the war years, when locals were keen to seek out affordable entertainment against a backdrop of worldwide turmoil. Neilly followed up his match-winning performance against the 'Hi-Hi' with a crashing equaliser against a St Mirren side watched by over 20,000 at Love Street. Morton's defence had been immense during this tricky away encounter and Mochan had scored following a newly-introduced free-kick routine after being laid on by Jimmy Whyte. Aberdeen then proved too strong at a packed Pittodrie and ran out winners by three goals to one. But again it was Neilly Mochan's venomous left boot that supplied the consolation goal for the Greenock side.

Within a month of the new campaign kicking off, Morton's inexperienced outside-left-cum-centre was being singled out by managers all over the country as a dangerous attacking threat. Cathkin Park and a brace in a four-goal draw were next up for Neilly as he wowed the 20,000 crowd with a solo burst for his first and a deceptive overhead flick in the lead-up to his second, taking his, and Morton's, tally for the season to six. At the time the Ton were suffering a 2-0 reverse against St Mirren at Cappielow on 9th October 1948, Celtic manager Jimmy McGrory was widely reported to have travelled to Middlesbrough with the intention of signing English international inside-forward Wilf Mannion. This was a player who was regarded "as great as Pele, perhaps even greater," by England team-mate Nat Lofthouse. Despite offering two players and a substantial sum of cash, McGrory travelled back to Glasgow without his man. When Celtic finally did splash out £12,000, it was on Clyde poacher Leslie Johnston. This as Scotland's most exciting striking prospect, Mochan, continued his sparkling form with another double, this time in a 3-1 win over Aberdeen.

Smiler Mochan, as the Scottish press were now referring to him, had scored all but one of Morton's League Cup goals, and work-rate had been a noticeable factor in his early success. Entertaining on the ball and with a deceptive turn of pace that often left opposing defenders waiting on an offside call, Neilly had tormented goalkeepers with a rocketing left-foot shot that had already become his trademark. McGrory and Celtic had missed the boat on this occasion as Mochan remained moored at the Tail o' The Bank.

Neilly, a non-smoking fitness fanatic, had returned from his national service as a strong and seemingly unstoppable unit with legs that moved like pistons when in striking distance. In considering his new-found footballing success, did those who knew him best see any change in Neilly's attitude? "He was a quiet guy really," said brother Denis. "If we went anywhere like a family wedding and people would come up and say, 'Hello uncle Neil', he'd say, 'Oh hello', then he'd turn around to me and ask, 'Who was that?' We spoke about football all the time but he would never speak about himself or what was happening where he was playing, he would just change the subject. He was a very kind person and his interests away from football were his family and the greyhounds. He was a great dog enthusiast and I think he must have taken his interest from our father. The other three of us never went to the dogs or anything but our dad was a whippet man and had done the dogs in his early days. Our father was an old-style bookie's runner and I used to run to the pub when I was young and get the lines and then run back to the house. My mother sat and did the nom de plumes and then the bets went in a clock bag and they went in at a minute to two. Then it was back into the pub, where my dad and six or seven others would go away to the 'Shire games. Neilly would do his dogs on a Friday night in Falkirk. Afterwards he'd come down to my mother's house and if Neilly had a good night at the dogs, all the ladies of the house were smiling; he was good to them all. He'd shout my mother through from the kitchen and slip something in the pocket of her apron. Neilly wasn't a drinker himself but if you went to his house, he'd pour drink for everyone else into big tumblers. He loved dancing as well and he'd maybe go to the dancing once a month. He'd get a whisky and lemonade when he got in and only have two over the whole night."

The scourge of the promising Scottish footballer has for generations been an over-indulgent taste for alcohol but, as nephew James Butler explains, Neilly never allowed himself to be caught up in the perils of such a vice. "The majority of folk would say that he didn't drink at all but now and again, if you could get him in the right mood, he would sit and have a whiskey and lemonade, maybe a couple. This was in his later years and even then you would maybe only see him drinking once a year. Neilly never went to the pub during his entire playing career. If someone went to visit him though, he'd put the cork in the bucket and start pouring drinks for them.

"He was fearless on the park and very shy in some respects off it. I think he got his build and hardy nature from his dad. People were scared of my grandfather, and it was no wonder when you saw the size of him, but the other Mochans weren't really like that. I think my grandad took that side of his character from his mother's family, the McLaughlans. They were from Buncrana and had an entirely different nature to the Mochans. Patrick McLaughlan, Neilly's cousin, was actually signed with Celtic in the '50s and his other cousin, John McLaughlan, was a prolific goalscorer for Clyde, Morton, Millwall and Dunfermline, so they had football blood in the family as well. My grandfather may have got a reputation as a hard man but he was only fighting his corner and I remember once he hit this guy outside the Carron Bar and knocked him out before promptly jumping on the bus home. When the other boy came round he was dishevelled and exclaiming to the crowd that had gathered, 'Rocky Marciano's in town tonight!' My grandfather was arrested in Hope Street in Falkirk as soon as he stepped off the bus and ended up spending the night in the cells."

Unafraid to battle like his father before him, on the football field at least, Neilly found himself entrenched in a relegation fight by the turn of the year. Morton had begun failing almost as badly as the waterlogged Cappielow pitch, which by the winter resembled a quagmire. The conditions at Neilly's home venue had been a problem for years and he used this to his benefit on at least one occasion in his early career. As a 17-year-old Morton hopeful during wartime, he would have to travel to the unofficial league matches by train. James Butler's father often drove Neilly to Greenock and an encounter against Rangers was particularly memorable. "My father told me the story of when came up against Willie Woodburn, who he described as being 'terrifying'," explained James Butler. "The pitch was a mess and there was a big puddle on the surface. The first thing that Woodburn said to Neilly was, 'You better not come near me because I'll break your legs,' and of course that didn't have any effect on him even at 17-years-old. A few minutes into the match and they both went for a high ball. Neilly just gave Woodburn a wee nudge on the leg and it knocked him off balance and head first into the puddle. Apparently there was a level of respect between the pair of them after that and they got on well throughout their careers."

A 4-1 trouncing at Ibrox on 11th December 1948 followed defeats from Albion Rovers, Hearts and East Fife, and left Morton languishing in 12th place of this 16-team division. Although Mochan had continued to stand out and regularly find the net, the state of the Cappielow playing surface was to massively undermine the club's survival prospects. Morton's home stadium, which mysteriously flew the flag of Greece in the 1940s, was closed down after a Scottish Cup replay against Inverness Caley due to the unplayable state of its pitch and Morton were forced to fulfil their remaining home fixtures at Love Street, Paisley, and Somerset Park, Ayr. Even alongside international stalwarts, no-one did more than Neilly in attempting to keep this Morton team from the unthinkable drop. By the time he travelled to Tynecastle in mid-March, Mochan had hit 12 goals, and another brace in Edinburgh inspired his struggling team to an unlikely 4-1 victory. Six days later and another double for Neilly against East Fife had *The Sunday Post* calling him a "chunky lump of human dynamite". "No wonder they call him 'Smiler'," the report added. "He shot over the bar and past the post. He tried it on his tummy and a lot of other peculiar positions but he finished up with two priceless goals. No more than just reward for the hardest afternoon's work I've seen in a long time. Mochan's ceaseless endeavour typifies the play of a Morton outfit fired on resolution to escape relegation."

A hat-trick against bottom-of-the-table Albion Rovers had Mochan on 19 goals for the season by the middle of April, and Morton were fighting it out with Clyde and Aberdeen to avoid finishing second-bottom. The player who marked Neilly for the Coatbridge side was Jock Stein, who was Rovers' best player that day. With Cowan in inspirational form at the back and Mochan hitting scorching drives past virtually every team he came up against, it was clear that these two players were the leading lights in the club's last-ditch fight to stave off relegation. *The Sunday Post* described the latter's goal in the 2-2 draw with title challengers Dundee as being "a ball hit so hard it almost tore the 'keeper's arm off." It was Neilly's 22nd goal from just 31 starts, and it came in front of the onlooking manager of Liverpool, George Kay.

A crowd of 35,000 watched as Morton finally succumbed to relegation at Love Street by the sword of eventual treble-winners Rangers. The club's

23-goal Mochan was soon out of contract, making it clear that he did not relish the prospect of second-tier football the following season. With a record to match Scotland's first-choice striker of that period, Queen of the South 's Billy Houliston, Neilly was deservedly regarded in the same bracket as top-class contemporaries such as Rangers' Willie Thornton, Clyde's Alec Linwood and Hearts' Willie Bauld. The romantic story of Billy Steel's discovery had captured Scottish football's imagination and the first club to table a bid for Neilly was misfiring Motherwell, who had finished their league campaign just three points ahead of Morton. If the claret and amber didn't arouse Neilly's interests, the rumours sweeping through the west of Scotland on 4th June 1949 surely would: Celtic had contacted Morton for a price and wished to sign him. The fee quoted was £12,000 and this was also being considered by Aberdeen, while St Mirren tabled a modest £9,000 offer. Mochan himself seemed unperturbed by the bidding frenzy and promptly booked a three-week holiday to Buncrana in Ireland with his close friend and Morton team-mate Tom McGarrity. Almost as soon as the pair left on their voyage to the Emerald Isle, Morton sold Colin Liddell to Hearts for £10,000. Not that this put Motherwell or Celtic off the Smiler's scent as Derby County, Newcastle United, Bury and Hull City also showed an interest.

As representatives from top British clubs travelled to Greenock with cheque books in tow, the ever-humble Mochan was able to reflect on an astonishing debut season while taking time out on a low-key post-season break. With the hampering war years and conscription behind him, Neilly had been able to make a monumental impact in a struggling side. He may rightly have wondered whether Morton, relegated just a year after their remarkable Scottish Cup run of 1948 and with a habit of selling their most lauded talents, matched his ambitions. Plenty of suitors had made their move but Neilly did not seem overly enthused about a move to England. So would his dream of moving to Celtic Park become a reality? Hoops fans were keen, as was Neilly, but he ultimately signed on for another year at Morton upon returning from Ireland.

And so it came to pass that Neilly Mochan would remain the darling of The Wee Dublin End for at least another season. Morton's top goalscorer at least knew that he would be pulling on the blue-and-white hoops at the club's own stadium after half a season of squatting in Paisley and Ayr. Nonetheless, with top sides north and south of the border scouting his every move, it always seemed a temporary solution. The question on every Scottish football writer's lips was, 'How much longer will Smiler Mochan call the sodden trenches of Cappielow home?'

Neilly's goals shot Morton straight back into the top league and Jim Davies had to fight off big-money bids from Manchester City and Preston for a player who was touted all season for a Scotland cap whilst playing in the second tier of Scottish football. The Preston chairman, Jim Taylor travelled to Carronshore to meet Neilly, who thought about his offer before writing to him with a refusal. One of his personal highlights of the 1949-50 campaign was during a 7-1 defeat of Alloa Athletic on 4th September 1949 when he scored five with three of his goals coming in just over two minutes. The 33-goal striker went into a charity match against Celtic for an Airdrie Select on 20th April 1950 as the hottest prospect in Scottish football and marked the occasion by scoring four goals in a 'come-and-get-me' performance.

Celtic failed to make their move and were punished again the following season when Mochan scored his famous hat-trick in Paradise. In another excellent performance during the 1950-51 campaign Neilly ran the show against Rangers at Ibrox but his Morton side still succumbed to a 2-0 defeat. "Mochan was outstanding," reported *The Sunday Post*. "The 30,000 crowd will remember the centre-forward display of Neilly Mochan, who looked Scotland class both on and off the ball. A pugnacious pimpernel, whose darts right, left and centre had the opposition almost crazy. If ever a man deserved to score, Neilly did."

The 'pugnacious pimpernel' nickname didn't stick but Smiler Mochan was clearly going places. With another impressive term securing Morton their top-flight status, and with the Cappielow board looking to fit the bill for stadium repairs, it was only a matter of time before Neilly was sold on. Against his better judgement, his transfer would take him to the North East of England.

CHAPTER 4:

A BORO BALLYHOO

David Jack was a world record-holder for four years in the late 1920s and early '30s when he became the most expensive footballer on the planet. Arsenal paid Bolton Wanderers almost £11,000 for the prolific inside-forward, who had a habit of creating history. Earlier in his career, Jack had netted the first ever goal at Wembley Stadium when he opened the scoring for Bolton against West Ham in the 1923 FA Cup Final. By Friday 8th May 1951 he had moved into management and made even more headlines as boss of Middlesbrough when he shelled out a sizeable £14,000 for Morton's Neilly Mochan. So keen was Jack to finally sign Billy Steel's protégé that, three days earlier, he had driven up to Carron personally to convince Neilly that his future lay at Ayresome Park. The Teessiders had kicked off the previous campaign in style and looked to be one of the leading lights of the First Division, as the top tier was then known, recording emphatic scorelines such as an 8-0 demolition of Huddersfield Town and a 7-3 decimation of Charlton Athletic. One of England's most celebrated players, Wilf Mannion, was the darling of the Boro support and they also boasted the talents of Scotsman Alex McCrae at inside-forward, Kingston-born striker Lindy Delapenha, centre-forward Johnny Spuhler and Italian goalkeeper and ex-Celt Rolando Ugolini. But the goals dried up at the turn of 1951 and a run of just four wins in 19 matches left Middlesbrough languishing in sixth position as Tottenham Hotspur went on to win the league championship.

The Teessiders desperately needed a proven goalscorer if they were to build on their impressive start to the 1950-51 campaign, and David Jack had to utilise all of his persuasion techniques to capture Mochan, who had previously made clear that a move to England held no attraction. Neilly enjoyed his home comforts and, at 24, had lived his entire life in the Falkirk area, save for his enforced two years' national service. His holidays normally involved a two-week break to Ireland and he was never far from the Mochan family unit. Nonetheless, while Celtic would have been Neilly's preferred destination, no offer was forthcoming and he agreed to move down south like so many Morton stars before him.

Over 30 years later, Albion Rovers striker Bernie Slaven would face a similar dilemma when he moved from Castlemilk to Middlesbrough at the same age of 24. As such, he identified with Mochan's misgivings and the challenges that followed. "When I went to England, although I was 24, I was immature and I didn't want to leave Glasgow," said Slaven. "I wondered what kind of club Middlesbrough would be and what the people and town would be like. When I was signing for Boro, my late father told me that the first guy I had to get a picture with was Wilf Mannion. I'd never heard of him at the time but he'd been nicknamed 'The Golden Boy' and played for England against Scotland at Hampden Park. I was coming from Albion Rovers, who were probably the worst team in Britain at that time, so arriving in England and having to get used to a new environment was a big transition for me.

"Coming from north of the border, it took me some time to adapt and after about three or four weeks I was on the phone to my father wanting to go home, even though I had trebled my wages at the time. I told my dad that I wasn't enjoying it, I didn't like the place and I was coming back home. But he said, 'What are you on about? You're not getting in here. Man up, you've only been there for three weeks. Give yourself a season and take it from there.' That was the best bit of advice I got from my father. If it wasn't for him, I would have gone back.

"One benefit is that the North East of England is not that far from home and you're only a two-and-a-half hour train journey back up. I was so unsettled during my first season that I was on that train back to Glasgow after every Middlesbrough game. It didn't matter whether I scored or not or if we were good, bad or indifferent, I went home and then got on the last train out of Glasgow Central station late on a Sunday to get back down for training on a Monday. It was a total waste of time and expenditure but it was my way of trying to adapt and keep sane. I found it difficult. Other guys can move about like travellers up and down the country and not bat an eyelid.

"My father was a Celtic diehard and knew everything about them. When I was coming down to Middlesbrough, he mentioned Neilly Mochan and told me he had made that transition from Scotland too. You have to consider though, that when Neilly came to Middlesbrough it would have been even darker down here with all the industry the place had. By the time I came down things were teetering out on Teesside and the factories were shutting down. Neilly would need to have worn a gas mask down here in the fifties with all the smog. They call us 'the smoggies' down here. Even when I arrived I remember coming down on the train and seeing these big towers with the smoke and chemicals and thinking that I had landed on the moon. God knows what Neilly would have thought when he went all those years before me as it would have been even darker back then and the air wouldn't have been as clear as when I got here."

Before sampling the thick Teesside air, Neilly took another unexpected break to his favoured destination of Buncrana in Ireland. He had a love affair with this part of the country that would last for many more years and it was during the close-season of 1951-52 that he was able to rekindle his friendship with John Langan, who had been his Cappielow comrade as a boy back in 1944. This reaquaintance was a stroke of luck and the holiday was a memorable prelude to Neilly's first season as a top-flight footballer in England, as Langan explained. "After I left Morton, some time passed before I met Neilly again. He had made a career for himself in Greenock and ended up being transferred to Middlesbrough and it was in that year that I met up with him. I was one of about 12 single men who were members of the Saint Mary's Church Social Club and we all decided that we would go to Buncrana in Ireland for a holiday. One of the boys who was coming with us was Hugh Mulhearn and he was cousins with Morton inside-left, Tommy McGarrity. Hugh and Tommy met at a family occasion and they decided that Tommy would come along to Buncrana with us and that he would bring two of his friends, one of whom was his former team-mate, Neilly Mochan.

"We went away for a fortnight and two of the lads were instrumentalists in bands. During the day we would be on the beach and those two would be playing the music and we would all be singing along. We would also take a ball down and kick it about all day and so the holiday was going well. Despite being at Cappielow with Neilly during the war, this was the first time I had actually seen him playing football. At Morton, we had only met at night and there was no ball work or anything like that.

"The nightlife was in the church hall. The attraction was that they had a good four-piece band and there were plenty of girls coming from all over on the first night of our holiday. Unfortunately for us, an old lady died in Buncrana and the parish priest said that he was shutting the dance hall for two nights as an act of respect. That put us out but we decided to go up to the Corinthian in Derry as we heard that it was a right good dance hall. We went up in various taxis and got split up. My cab took us straight into the dancing and the car that Neilly was travelling in ended up heading somewhere else so the boys could get a refreshment. In those days of the dancing, the girls normally stood at one side of the hall and the boys stood on the other but when we got into the Corinthian we noticed that girls were standing on both sides of the hall. After a dance we sort of ascertained that one group of girls was Catholic and the other was Protestant. We were dancing away in any case when one of the doormen came in and tapped me on the shoulder and asked, 'Are those your friends outside? You better come out here because one of them is singing Celtic songs and was calling us all the Masonic bastards for not letting them in.'

"That was the end of our first night and we bundled ourselves back to Buncrana in taxis. The following evening the barman at the hotel told us about another dance hall on the outskirts so we decided to go there. On the road up we asked one of the drivers if there was a local pub but there wasn't one. They explained that if we wanted a drink then we could visit this old woman who made pot whiskey. One of the cars headed straight to the dancing and the other went to test the homemade whiskey. So half-a-dozen of us arrived at the dance hall and there wasn't another man in there. The girls had so much cosmetics on that you would have thought that someone had hit them with a flour bag. We were up dancing with these girls and the band started playing 'White Christmas' and this was the middle of summer. Just as we thought that things couldn't get much worse, the local boys started filtering into the hall. You could see that some of them had come straight in from the fields as they still had their work boots on. Neilly's cab arrived just as this crowd started to come in and there was a bit of an atmosphere because we were up dancing with all the local girls. Before anything could happen to us, two of the natives fell out and started fighting amongst themselves in the middle of the hall. Everybody seemed to know the drill and stood up on the seats to watch as if they were ringside at a big fight. They fought until one of them had enough and then 'White Christmas' came back on and we all started dancing again but it was obvious that our presence wasn't approved of. We could sense a nasty atmosphere and decided that we better get out of there but we couldn't convince Neilly because he was really enjoying the dancing. We eventually got out and the boys came after us. We were running down the street and they were chasing us and throwing stones and boulders and then an open-backed lorry came out of nowhere and stopped. The driver asked if we were in trouble and told us to jump on the back of his vehicle. Even with the stench and all the dirt we were happy to make our escape on the back of that lorry and that was the end of another night.

"Despite all of this we still had a great holiday and one day we stayed in the boarding house because it was raining. The two lads were playing their instruments and another boy was a bit of a comedian and he was doing all these impressions. Neilly's character really came out that day. He was lying on the bed holding his sides with laughter shouting at the comedian, 'Stop it, my stomach's hurting.' He was really enjoying himself and that was Neilly's sense of humour. He loved a good laugh. It was no wonder they called him Smiler Mochan."

From the tomfoolery of Buncrana, Neilly soon made the train journey down to Middlesbrough for the serious business of his Ayresome Park introduction. KF Partizan Beograd were in their infancy and just six years old when the Yugoslavians travelled to Teesside as part of the Festival of Britain celebrations. The UK government had organised a series of events throughout the country to instil a sense of post-war recovery and galvanisation across the nation and sporting encounters were an integral feature of this national jamboree. In Scotland, the Corporation of Glasgow organised a football tournament and named it after the Patron Saint of the city, Saint Mungo. In England there were a series of exhibition matches between British and continental sides. As Celtic prepared to contest the one-off Saint Mungo Cup, which they were to win in the aftermath of their 16th Scottish Cup success, Mochan made his Middlesbrough debut on 12 May 1951 against this unusual team from Belgrade.

In the years before European football tournaments, such friendly matches offered an air of mystique and wonderment, and an impressive 30,000 turned out to witness Mochan's debut against the Yugoslavs, who included the legendary striker Stjepan Bobek. The Yugoslavian internationalist was the best player on the Ayresome Park pitch that afternoon in May and went on to score over 400 competitive goals in less than 500 games for Partizan.

Although Middlesbrough were overturned 3-2, Neilly got on the score-sheet and set up his side's other goal. His impact had been immediate and hinted at a resolution to the goalscoring problems that had dented Middlesbrough's silverware quest in their previous campaign. "There was plenty to be pleased about in the performance of Mochan," the *Hartlepool Mail* wrote of the striker's first appearance "The powerfully-built leader looks a big improvement on what Boro have."

Neilly was not the only Mochan making a move in the football world during the summer of 1951, as younger brother Willie made the transition from Camelon Juniors to Bob Shankly's Falkirk. The 22-year-old outside-left had also attracted interest from Alloa, Stenhousemuir and Morton before signing on at Brockville. Like his elder sibling, Willie had a penchant for cannonball shots and Shankly hoped that his impressive shooting and crossing prowess could lift his hometown club out of Division B at the first time of asking.

As Willie made headway in the lower reaches of Scottish football, Neilly's first taste of the English game came against champions Tottenham Hotspur at Ayresome Park. Middlesbrough's curtain-raiser ended in a surprising 2-1 victory for the home side and the Scottish forward marked his arrival by playing a vital part in Boro's equalising goal. Mochan described his inside-forwards, Wilf Mannion and Alex McCrae as "outstanding players" and, buoyed by their victory against the best side in England, the Ayresome Park faithful finally believed they had found the man to complement this duo's apparent abilities. This new-found optimism was short-lived however, and if ever a match epitomised Mochan's time in English football, it was the one that came four days later at Old Trafford. The striker scored a memorable brace against Matt Busby's first championship-winning side but the suspect travelling defence leaked twice as many, and Middlesbrough lost the game 4-2. These frailties would prove a recurring theme throughout the season for David Jack's side and, despite the undoubted individual talents of Mannion, Delapenha, McCrae and Fitzsimons, Middlesbrough lacked the cohesion and consistency required to build on the previous season's top-six finish. Often starved of service, Mochan was regularly utilised in other areas of the pitch and was occasionally dropped when his team's performances hit the buffers.

Six matches in September 1951 yielded three victories and three defeats, and a topsy-turvy maiden season for Neilly ensued. He got among the goals, scoring in a 5-0 defeat of Burnley, a 2-0 win over Fulham and twice against West Bromwich Albion as Middlesbrough ran out 3-2 winners at the Hawthorns. But these efforts were cancelled out by a 3-1 defeat to the great Nat Lofthouse's Bolton, a 4-3 reverse at Charlton and a narrow 1-0 loss to Huddersfield. By the time of Chelsea's scoreless draw at Ayresome Park in October, the Middlesbrough fans signalled their dismay with a slow and lengthy hand-clap after 70 minutes in protest at their side's indifferent early-season displays.

On 13th October 1951, Mochan found the net again, and led his new team's scoring chart on seven goals for the season. Middlesbrough scored four that day at Fratton Park but still failed to emerge with so much as a point, as Portsmouth netted five. Following a poor result such as this, David Jack thought nothing of making sweeping changes to his side, and as many as six alterations from match to match was a regular indication of his struggle to find a winning blend. Neilly continued to impress, often at outside-left, and got on the score sheet again at the end of the month, this time against Stanley Matthews' Blackpool in a 2-2 draw. Adaptable and tenacious as he was, Neilly Mochan could not raise Middlesbrough from the doldrums, and November 1951 proved a bleak month for his struggling side. Defeats to Arsenal, Manchester City and Danny Blanchflower's Aston Villa could not be offset by a solitary point at home to Derby County as the pressure mounted on the Boro boss.

Back in Scotland, Willie Mochan was out of favour at Brockville and was transferred to East Stirlingshire as Bob Shankly audaciously signed former Celt, Jimmy Delaney, from Aberdeen. As the Mochan brothers' fortunes seemed to stutter in the winter of 1951, two players who were to feature prominently in the elder sibling's future career were also making headlines. While John McPhail considered a coaching offer from the Eastern States of America that would enrich him with a £3,000 annual bounty, his Celtic bosses made a surprise signing on 4th December 1951. The Glasgow side had suffered a centre-half injury crisis and brought in former Albion Rovers stopper, Jock Stein, as cover from Welsh side Llanelly. At the time of this somewhat unspectacular purchase, Jimmy McGrory offered Celtic's downbeat rationale as he explained, "We have to make sure of having an experienced man standing by." Little did McGrory realise that Stein would never be content with being a standby, and the decision to sign the ex-Blantyre Vics Junior would prove to be the greatest piece of business in the history of the club.

As Stein settled into Celtic Park, the freefall of Mochan's Middlesbrough continued as they plummeted to 20th place in the English First Division following a 4-0 hammering at Wolves. Neilly was rarely utilised in the centre-forward position where he had established such a prolific reputation, despite his side always looking better when he was switched to this central role. After further defeats at White Hart Lane and then at home to Preston, Neilly was dropped for the Boxing Day clash against Stoke. This practice became the norm for the following season-and-a-half at Ayresome Park, with the big-money striker becoming something of a scapegoat for the often dire performances of his underachieving team-mates. A return to the side for Neilly at Turf Moor resulted in a goal against Burnley, but a humiliating 7-1 reverse meant he was missing for the first match of 1952.

At a crossroads in his career, Mochan's goalscoring prowess had not been forgotten north of the border, and Aberdeen - keen to replace the recently departed Delaney - immediately made enquiries about Smiler. The forward was so out of the picture at Middlesbrough that he was in Stirling on 23 January 1952 as a spectator for Albion's home game against St Mirren. When asked by one eagle-eyed reporter if he was keen to swap the Boro red for Aberdeen's, Neilly claimed that he knew nothing of the move. "He used to tell me to lie to people," nephew Jimmy Butler explained. "He always said that if someone asks you something that you don't want to speak to them about then you should just tell them lies and let them believe whatever they want to." It would appear that Mochan had been up to his usual capers with the Annfield press-man as Aberdeen had indeed offered to match the price that the Ayresome Park club paid for him just eight months before. The English side wanted £1,000 more and Aberdeen boss, Dave Halliday, ceased his pursuit of the unsettled player. It had been the Pittodrie side's second serious offer for the Carron-born striker as they had failed in a £30,000 double swoop for him and Morton team-mate Jimmy Mitchell when Mochan was the toast of the 'Ton.

The attraction of a Stirling Albion Wednesday night fixture wasn't the sole reason for Neilly's trip home. He had also started courting a young lady from Maddiston, near Falkirk, called Mary McAuley. "I loved dancing from a young age," reminisced the future Mrs Mochan. "When I was younger I used to do Highland and tap-dancing and when I left the school I got into the ballroom dancing. I first met Neil at Doaks dancehall in Falkirk. He spotted me across the dance hall and I spotted him. It was love at first sight with my husband and I. I can still picture that moment in the dancehall. After that first night we met, Neil and I would see each other at the dancing and he would dash over to ask me for a dance." This was a true and enduring romance and, though Neilly's football club was down on Teesside, his heart remained in Falkirk.

"They were married in 1952 in Falkirk," reminisced James Butler. "The evening reception was at Mathiesons dancehall in the High Street. I remember that some of his ex-Morton team-mates were there and Jimmy Whyte went into Woolworths with Jimmy Cowan and came out with all this lipstick. I was a horrified seven-year-old, looking on as my uncle Neilly was covered in lippy and they were rolling up his trousers and all sorts of nonsense. Whyte was the biggest culprit but I remember Neilly told me that he was always up to his tricks at Morton. Back in those days, if they were playing away from home they didn't just share a room in a hotel; they shared a bed as well. Jimmy would deliberately wear silk pyjamas and when his team-mate got into bed he would put his arm around him. That was his way of making sure he got the bed to himself."

While out of the first-team for a month at the beginning of 1952, Neilly would have the opportunity to see his second-youngest brother, John, representing Scotland in a youth international match against England at Roker Park. John was a skilful inside-right who plied his trade with Menstrie Vics and there were high hopes that the third of the Mochan boys would also make the grade at senior level. During Neilly's absence from the Middlesbrough side, the Teessiders suffered another two distressing defeats when Fulham destroyed them 6-0 at Craven Cottage and Doncaster Rovers put four passed them on their own patch. It was blatantly clear that Neilly Mochan was not the cause of Boro's slump but he was recalled only intermittently as his side finished a disappointing 19th in the league. In his first 30 appearances in English football, Neilly had scraped together 12 goals and had regularly scored four or five goals-a-game when demoted to the reserves. This could perhaps be considered a reasonable return in a side fighting relegation but Mochan himself was not convinced as he analysed his first season in Teesside in '50s magazine *Charles Buchan's Football Monthly*. "I played mostly at centre-forward, flanked by two fine inside-men in Wilf Mannion and Arthur Fitzsimons. This English-Scottish-Irish combination should have sparkled but somehow I could not match up to the other two. I couldn't get among the goals. And that, of course, is what English leaders are expected to do. In Scotland I had been used to an entirely different style of play. Scots players and teams tend to try and work and scheme their openings and the pace is certainly slower. The first thing I discovered in England was that you must never be caught in possession. The ball has to be moved quickly and smartly and openings must be created by the pass, giving the defender no time to turn back or jockey for position. In Scotland, where dribbling is still part of the game, an inside-forward is allowed the time and space to try to beat one or more opponents before he slips through his pass. It's probably more academic to watch, but in England this type of play seldom pays off against quick-tackling defenders who are often faster off the mark than the forwards they are shadowing. That is the way I found it in the English First Division."

Mochan had left Morton one year earlier as one of Scotland's most promising players. He had already been selected for international squads and had a host of clubs to choose from when he decided to leave the Greenock side. His debut season in English football had not been the success many sportswriters and football fans would have expected and by the final months of the campaign, and with Middlesbrough fighting relegation, he had lost his first-team berth to Johnny Spuhler, the striker he had initially been purchased to replace. Despite a promising start to the 1952-53 season when Neilly regained his position at centre-forward and scored the only goal of the opening league encounter against Burnley, he was out of the side again after just four games. Banished to the reserves for most of the season, Mochan played just nine first-team matches and scored two goals. The writing was on the wall for the man known as Smiler, and the powerful forward explained his predicament. "In my second season I was not at all surprised to find myself spending as much time in the reserves as in the league side despite the handsome fee that Middlesbrough had paid Morton for me. By May 1953

I had more or less decided there was no future for me in England. During my two years with the First Division side I couldn't settle down; I seldom felt really happy with my game. And yet I was not disgruntled at Ayresome Park. Middlesbrough treated me very well and, in some ways, I was sorry to leave them."

As well as having to make a football decision, Neilly also had his private life to consider as he and Mary started a family. Their first child, John, arrived on 26th February 1953 and this, with his diminishing number of Middlesbrough appearances, may have contributed to the end of his football career in England.

Football correspondent Lee Norris called Mochan's failure at Middlesbrough a "mystery" in the 1950s football weekly magazine, *Soccer Star*. "Neil Mochan, the broad shouldered, thick set, bow legged little man. His rolling gait, his studied control of the ball, his cannonball left boot, his slyness of passing the ball," wrote Norris. "And yet it was this man I saw at Middlesbrough, a bewildered member of a fast-moving side, dilly-dallying about the field, flatfooted, and almost transfixed by all about him.

"Mochan was, frankly and honestly, one of the Middlesbrough misfits in the middle. Since the war the Ayresome Park club have slapped down cheques that have brought centre-forwards with fine sounding names. Yet once again this season they have had to go out and buy another, Ken McPherson. Mochan ranks alongside Andy Donaldson and Alex Linwood as men who have failed at Ayresome Park. They were the chosen men to follow the famous footsteps of George Camsell and Micky Fenton. They failed. It is the stranger when you consider that the game's greatest schemer at inside-forward wears Boro's colours - Wilf Mannion. Why did they fail?

"I will tell you the reason in the case of Mochan and the case of the other Scottish centre star, Linwood. English football demands an essentially typed sort of centre-forward. Scottish football gives the centre-forward more scope and more time. English football was too fast, too furious for the smiling Neil Mochan. Everyone knew him at Middlesbrough as the Smiler. He was just that. Although things were going wrong for him, he smiled pluckily through it. He played in the reserve team with great enthusiasm and didn't mind a spell or two on the left-wing for the First Division club.

"Although the crowds were not Mochan mad, they did hand it to him that he couldn't half hit a ball and he could play football. But he couldn't score enough goals and he couldn't make them as much as this soccer-crazy town wanted him to. Now, Middlesbrough fans know a good centre-forward when they see one. But it is only one type of middle man they like - a Wilson or an Elliott or Camsell or a Fenton - lively players who are packed with punch plus. Mochan did not fit into that category so he failed.

"That answers half the mystery. The other half is why then should he have succeeded in the tough, tense tussling of Scottish soccer? It might be easy to say that Scottish football is slower. I don't go for that one this time. Not one little bit. I grant you, a ball player, unless he is a Hagan or a Mannion or a Carter, which means if he is a genius, needs time on his hands to manoeuvre and frolic. But Mochan - and he would be the first to admit it - is not a genius. Very few footballers are. He is one of those men who make soccer for the greater, brighter stars. Moreover with Middlesbrough he was not expected to play a switching game with wing men and inside forwards.

That did not fit into the tactics of the Boro boys - tactics that have thrilled crowds all over England but never in fact won them anything. His job was in the middle. He could move about a bit but the players expected him to be in the middle when the ball came his way. Now, Mochan is a rover. A rover is only just as good as the team tactics will let him be. And there is not much room nowadays in English soccer for a wanderer."

The Middlesbrough team that Neilly Mochan joined had a wealth of talented individuals. Players such as Wilf Mannion, Lindy Delapenha and Arthur Fitzsimons were international-class stars who on their day could be match winners. However, the team failed to gel as a unit, were dreadfully weak in defence, and were ultimately unsuccessful over an entire league campaign. A similar dilemma would rear its head at Celtic Park throughout their inconsistent 1950s and it was in his beloved hoops that Mochan would finally fulfil his potential after a disappointing two years on Teesside. Having sampled the finest vintage that English football had to offer in the aforementioned Mannion, as well as Stanley Matthews, Nat Lofthouse and Danny Blanchflower, Neilly began spending more and more time back in his hometown as his football career derailed. "Middlesbrough had the makings of a good side and a young Brian Clough was just coming through," remembered Jimmy Butler. "Cloughie was Neilly's boot-boy and they got on well. But Neilly fell out of favour and came back up the road. He was sitting around Carron not doing very much. Then Celtic came calling and he never looked back."

CHAPTER 5:

THE MOCHAN CUP

"When the ball hits the net,
Like a vampire jet,
That's a-Mochan..."

To the tune of ***That's Amore*** by Dean Martin (1953)

Celtic had flirted with the prospect of signing Neilly Mochan as early as June 1949. The club's solitary subsequent success – the 1951 Scottish Cup - had done little to convince their long-suffering support of the wisdom in overlooking one of the country's most proficient goal-getters. The league form of Jimmy McGrory's charges had been nothing short of abysmal, as they finished fifth, seventh, ninth and eighth in the four seasons following their failure to purchase the then free-scoring Morton forward. The club had since struggled to find a prolific striker and largely relied on John McPhail's goals from 1949 until 1951. Since then, with McPhail reverting to a deeper role in this struggling Celtic side, their top goalscorers totalled just 13 strikes in 1952 and a paltry 11 in 1953. Even the left-field and groundbreaking signing of Jamaican Gilbert Heron had ultimately proven unsuccessful and news of Mochan's Middlesbrough morass had travelled as far as the East End of Glasgow.

Neilly himself described Celtic's approach in the post-season of 1952-

53 as "a big surprise," and went on to explain, "I was at home in Falkirk when I was visited by a Celtic scout who told me that Mr Jimmy McGrory, the Celts' manager, wanted to see me at Parkhead. That was on a Friday morning. In the afternoon I saw Mr McGrory, was told that Celtic and Middlesbrough had agreed on my transfer, and in a matter of moments became a Tims' player.

"Ever since I had been a boy in Camelon it had been my ambition to play for Celtic and, as boys do, I looked forward to the day, not that I believed it would really come, when I would score a hat-trick for the famous Glasgow club. I never visualised scoring one against my favourites. While I was in England, the first result I always looked for on Saturday evenings was Celtic's. You can imagine my delight, therefore, when the club I always wanted to join made a sudden offer for my transfer."

Four months of languishing in the Middlesbrough reserves had brought Neilly's value down considerably and, on Friday 8th May 1953, the fee the two clubs agreed on was £8,000. Neil Mochan's Celtic contract listed him as residing at his parents' address of 5 Park Crescent, Carronshore Road, by Falkirk, and the Minute of Agreement stated that Neilly would be paid, "£12 per week in the playing season and £11 per week in the closed season with an additional £2 per week when playing in the first team, subject to a bonus of £1 per point when playing in the first team and 10 shillings per point when playing in the second team." The two witnesses who enabled Mochan to seal his one-year contract were Celtic's secretary, Audrey Douglas, and groundsman, Charles Doherty.

Tragically, on the day Neilly was at Parkhead to sign for his boyhood heroes, an 18-year-old boy from Langside in Glasgow collapsed on the Celtic

Park pitch and died 15 minutes later. The prefect from St Aloysius Senior Secondary School had been participating in a schools' football match and had not been involved in any physical altercation leading up to his demise. Sadly, his two younger siblings had been in the crowd to support their big brother and looked on in despair as he was stretchered up the tunnel.

When Neilly's career derailed in Teesside, it would have been a remarkable test of character for the 26-year-old. The game is littered with players who have suffered such a period of disappointment and uncertainty and failed to recapture the glittering form that earned them their big-money transfer in the first place. A fractious belligerence can often creep into the footballer's psyche and prevent them from transforming their fortunes. But that wasn't part of Neilly's makeup. He realised that his talents, which had attracted suitors from all over Scotland and England just two years previously, would not desert him forever. He also certainly knew that there was no ignominy in a move to Celtic Park under any circumstances. During his bleaker months at Middlesbrough, Neilly had sought solace in his home town of Carron. The familiar ironworks, which stood a corner-kick's distance from his parents' home, had a seal on which was engraved three cannons below a nest engulfed by flames. The phoenix above those iron cannons evoked visions of rebirth and, for Mochan's first year at Celtic at least, the club would finally rise from its post-war malaise.

Numerous lavish celebrations, abhorrently lavish in nature, were already underway to celebrate the coronation of Queen Elizabeth II by the time Mochan arrived at Celtic Park. The coronation was estimated to have cost the British taxpayer over £1 million and, in protest, a left-winger of a political nature was prompted to produce an educational pamphlet entitled, 'The Crown and the Cash'. Welshman Emrys Hughes, a Labour MP for South Ayrshire and a son-in-law of Keir Hardie himself, stated in his controversial written piece that, "It soon became clear that the coronation of the new Queen was to be made the occasion for an enormously expensive spectacle." Hughes continued that the stands along the Queen's processional route were, "All part of the spectacle to hypnotise and make the people think in red, white and blue, the Tory election colours. Was there any need in these days of heavy taxation and calls for economy for such an elaborate coronation, half-ceremony, half-circus?" Many would believe that the red, white and blue referenced by Hughes, a self-confessed republican and anti-monarchist, would also adorn the Coronation Cup when eight British football teams, including Scottish double-winners Rangers, did battle for this prestigious one-off football tournament in Glasgow throughout the month of May.

Before competing in their Coronation Cup matches, Celtic and Rangers had to play their Glasgow Charity Cup Semi-Final ties against Third Lanark and Queen's Park respectively. Both matches ended in 1-1 draws and both were settled on the toss of a coin, with Celtic and Scottish B Division amateur side Queen's Park progressing by this least distinguished of methods. Celtic and Queen's Park had last met in the tournament's final back in 1937 and Celtic won that highly-entertaining encounter 4-3. This year's showpiece would take place at Hampden Park the day after Mochan signed for Celtic, and Smiler was thrown right into his first match and first cup final for his new side. It was expected that his appearance would add thousands to the Hampden Park gate, as the Celtic support seemed keen to witness this exciting new personality in action after suffering yet another trophyless campaign.

Jock Stein had been handed the captain's armband by the injured Sean Fallon and remembered preparing for Celtic's end of season matches when he spoke to Jim Craig during the Lisbon Lion's radio show *Cairney's Corner* in the early 1970s. "A week before it we went down to play against Ayr United in a game just to try and put a team together because it was obvious that the manager, Mr McGrory, wasn't happy with the side at that time and neither were the directors," recalled Stein. "I don't think they had any reason to be pleased with it and there was talk of different signings and such. We went down to play Ayr United and we lost that match 3-1 and that match certainly didn't do anything to help us. It put us back a bit. But we did sign Neil Mochan at that time, which made a big difference to us because we had a Charity Cup Final before the Coronation Cup and that was his debut for the club. He came in and did well and I think we all got a lift from that."

On 9th May 1953, thousands lined the streets of London to watch the state coach, in which the Queen and the Duke of Edinburgh were due to travel on 2 June, being used for the first time in a coronation rehearsal. On the same day, thousands more lined the Hampden Park terraces to get a glimpse of Neilly Mochan being fielded by Celtic for the first time in their very own coronation rehearsal. The line-ups for the 1953 Glasgow Charity Cup Final were:

Celtic: Bonnar; Haughney, Rollo; Evans, Stein, McPhail; Collins, Fernie, Mochan, Peacock, Tully
Queen's Park: Weir; Harnett, Stewart; Cromar, Bell, Hastie; Callan, O'Connell, Church, Dalziel, Omand

The scene was set and Mochan finally entered the stage adorned in Celtic's alluring green-and-white. In the opening exchanges of this cup final, contested in intense Hampden heat, Celtic had three excellent opportunities to open the scoring. Their supporters within the 46,000 strong crowd got an early glimpse of Mochan's cannonball left-footed shot as he sent a trademark drive just over the Queen's Park crossbar. On the half-hour mark, the new Bhoy displayed other facets of his game as his speed and control took him past two Queen's Park defenders and into a position to chip the ball almost from the goal-line into the path of the oncoming Willie Fernie. Fernie duly finished off an excellent move to put his side 1-0 up and virtually every member of the Celtic team rushed over to congratulate the debutant and creator of the opening goal. Moments later and Neilly was on the score sheet himself after being set up by Alex Rollo, and on 65 minutes he scored his second, albeit after blatantly controlling Bobby Collins' through ball with his arm. Mochan's sublime performance in his first appearance sent the rambunctious Celtic crowd home happy, even after Queen's Park pulled back a consolation through O'Connell three minutes from time. Two of Celtic's standouts, Mochan and goalkeeper John Bonnar, had found form just in time for the Coronation Cup. As Neilly said of his own performance, "In my first game in the famous green-and-white hoops I rediscovered my scoring touch."

It may have been argued that Mochan's contribution on his debut had been devalued by the lower-league opposition and that the real test would come against the top-class English sides that Celtic could face in the Coronation Cup. Neilly's detractors down south certainly wouldn't bet on him turning over the likes of English Division One champions Arsenal, or Matt Busby's Manchester United. One English football observer who had plenty to write about Neilly's spell in England was Lee Norris of football weekly, *Soccer Star*. "As a player Mochan is a happy character. He gives the impression of being a little carefree, a little haphazard," wrote Norris in one article "Maybe one of his greatest failings when he first came into English football was his inability to fight back. But on the move he is a hard man to knock off the ball. He has that roll of the shoulders that was one time Sailor Brown's own particular brand of body swerve. Mochan doesn't utilise it so freely or so cheekily as Brown did, but that is through lack of complete confidence in himself. Mochan is apologetic for his performance. You always feel as though he wants to stop and apologise every time he beats a player."

Neilly may not have fully convinced this English football writer of his credentials as a top-class footballer but the experience he gained in England's top flight was invaluable. Neilly had faced Arsenal, scored a brace against Manchester United at Old Trafford and made his debut against Tottenham Hotspur in the red of Middlesbrough. The only English side in the tournament he had not been acquainted with was Newcastle. Hibernian and Aberdeen would join Celtic and Rangers as the Scottish representatives in this eight-team knock-out tournament, and matches would be played at Ibrox Stadium and Hampden Park.

Before a royal ball was launched, the English and Scottish players' unions had forwarded a complaint to the Ministry of Labour over the players' terms during the Coronation Cup event and had requested an increase in fees for each player to £10 per match. The unions had also urged that a donation be made to their respective benevolent funds but Sir George Graham, the secretary of the organising committee, would not entertain such notions and the players ended up participating under protest.

Jock Stein spoke to Jim Craig about the tournament and remembered the obstinate opposition he and his team-mates faced in the lead-up to their opening fixture. "Johnny Hughes was the union official then and he felt that it was a big competition and there would be a lot of money drawn at the turnstiles, so we should be paid a guaranteed £10 for each match that we played in. There was some consultation between the players and the officials of each club but it never went to any great length. I think that Bob Kelly, the chairman at that time, brought us all in individually and asked us all our opinion of it. We all wanted to play in the competition but each club had to make their mind up. It wasn't as if the Scottish clubs would get together. The two Scottish clubs that were certain to be in it were Celtic and Rangers. There's no way we could make any decision between the Rangers players and ourselves but at the outset we were talking about strike. At the end of the day, with the pull of the big game, we all wanted to be in it and we were not willing to decide that we weren't going to play. The chairman did say at that time that it didn't matter who wouldn't play, there would be a Celtic team in the competition. It didn't matter where they came from, there would be a team with green-and-white jerseys on. It frightened quite a lot of the people then and it was quite easy, we were going to play."

And play they did, with a renewed vigour all too absent from Celtic sides of the late 1940s and early '50s. Celtic and Aberdeen's involvement in the tournament had been something of a surprise given their distinct lack of recent success compared to double-winners Rangers and Hibernian, who had won the Scottish League in 1951 and 1952. Of the English sides, Tottenham Hotspur had won the First Division in 1951, Manchester United had been invited to participate in the tournament as champions of England in 1952 and Arsenal had dispossessed them of their crown in 1953. Newcastle United had won the FA Cup twice in succession in 1951 and 1952. "I think Celtic's participation in it was purely financial," Stein told Jim Craig, "It was supposed to be the top two in the league first of all that would be in it and we didn't qualify but obviously Celtic's pull at the gate was important."

Celtic completely outclassed Arsenal, overwhelming tournament favourites, in the first-round match at Hampden Park on 11th May 1953, the 1-0 scoreline flattering the English champions. Bobby Collins scored the winning goal directly from a corner kick in the 23rd minute as Mochan's arrival continued to reinvigorate the Celtic side. John McPhail produced a first-class performance at wing-half; Jock Stein was impenetrable, commanding and assured at the back; Jimmy Walsh's speed caused Arsenal problems all evening; and Charlie Tully looked to be back to his irrepressible best. The Celtic contingent among the 59,500 crowd were able to enjoy this rare moment of glory as they witnessed their team transcend their wildest expectations against elite English opposition.

Celtic: Bonnar; Haughney, Rollo; Evans, Stein, McPhail; Collins, Walsh, Mochan, Peacock, Tully
Arsenal: Swindin; Wade, Chenhall; Forbes, Dodgin, Mercer; Roper, Goring, Holton, Lishman, Marden

On the same evening, Tottenham Hotspur played on Scottish turf for the first time in their history as they met Hibernian in front of 45,000 at Ibrox. Gordon Smith's ninth-minute opener was cancelled out by Sonny Walters and the replay went ahead the very next night on the same bare and bumpy pitch. Only 15,000 turned out for the second match as both sides selected unchanged line-ups. Lawrie Reilly scored twice after Sid McClellan had put the Londoners ahead, and Hibernian's victory - like Celtic's before it - poured scorn on that apocryphal belief that Scottish football sides were weaker than their English counterparts. The Scots had drawn first blood in the first two games as Spurs endured the same fate as their city neighbours and joined Arsenal on the long coach journey home.

The remaining first-round fixtures were played on 13th May 1953 and proved far more favourable for the English sides. A crowd of 75,000 was at Hampden to watch Manchester United knock Rangers out with a 2-1 scoreline and allay any fears that Emrys Hughes may have had concerning red, white and blue ribbons being tied to the Coronation Cup. In the final first-round tie, Newcastle, with Ronnie Simpson in goal, trounced beaten Scottish Cup finalists Aberdeen 4-0 in front of a threadbare 5,000 crowd at Ibrox. Manchester United had emerged as the new favourites to win the tournament and their semi-final tie paired them with the giant-killers of the first round, Celtic.

Neilly had left his troubles behind in Teesside and, within just 180 minutes, this frequently dismal Celtic side had augmented its powers with his inclusion. His success had also percolated through the writings of *Soccer Star's* Lee Norris. "Now Mochan is back there (in Scotland) and back has come the sun in a soccer star's career," wrote Norris. "Mochan must do a lot of great things before he will rank as one of the best centre-forwards in Scotland. But he has that characteristic solidity of the Scot - to take the rough with the smooth. And Neil has had quite a bit of both recently. He plays his soccer with thorough enjoyment, he revels in a struggle and as his confidence comes seeping back he will play with an even cheekier grin and a broader smile. His football has a giggle in it. But there is nothing very funny in the way he hits a ball with his left foot. Give him a ball rolled back on his left foot and Mochan almost wriggles with delight. He catches it with a delight he cannot conceal. And if it rockets into the back of the net there hasn't been a planet discovered yet that is too high for him to jump over."

Celtic's clash with the slayers of Rangers was scheduled for Hampden, and Neilly Mochan would attain the unique distinction of playing his first three matches for Celtic at the national stadium. Mochan had breathed new life into this underachieving group of players but it would be a monumental achievement to continue such exalted form against Matt Busby's impressive Manchester United. Neilly had recent experience of playing against the Old Trafford outfit for Middlesbrough and this would prove pivotal as Celtic plotted the downfall of these Mancunian titans.

A huge crowd was expected for this semi-final tie but some of the tournament attendances thus far had been nothing short of desolate. Receipts for each fixture, less expenses, would be split up with 25 per cent each being paid to the competing clubs and the remaining 50 per cent being disseminated between the King George VI Memorial Fund, The National Playing Fields Association and the Central Council of Physical Recreation. A farrago of prestige and profit was surely at the heart of Bob Kelly's decision to put a team, any team, out to represent Celtic in this competition.

The cacophony of 73,000 spectators swirled around Hampden Park, carried by a strong Glasgow gale, as Celtic faced Manchester United on 16th May 1953. Celtic's wing-halves, Bobby Evans and John McPhail, did more than anyone to garner another unexpected but well-deserved victory against the cream of English football. Evans consistently covered for McPhail, whose passing was beguiling in its accuracy and vision. Mochan, for his part, was up against Allenby Chilton and relentlessly dragged the England cap from one side of the pitch to the other as Celtic tirelessly worked to build on their first-round success. On 24 minutes, Charlie Tully nonchalantly chipped a pass on to countryman Bertie Peacock, whose powerful drive opened the scoring. Eight minutes into the second half and it was Tully again who expertly controlled a Rollo pass and delivered it over Chilton's head and on to Mochan, whose run was timed to perfection. Jack Crompton advanced from the United goal to meet the onrushing Celtic forward but Neilly rifled a right-footed shot into the corner of the net to put Celtic two ahead and score his third goal for the club in three games. The prolific England internationalist, Jack Rowley, pulled a goal back for United 13 minutes from time but Celtic held on to win 2-1 and progress to the final to face either Hibernian or Newcastle United. The Hoops fans were ecstatic and proudly waved flags of Eire around the national stadium - an act that was described by *The Glasgow Herald* as, "inopportune to say the least."

Celtic: Bonnar; Haughney, Rollo; Evans, Stein, McPhail; Collins, Walsh, Mochan, Peacock, Tully
Manchester United: Crompton; McNulty, Aston; Carey, Chilton, Gibson; Viollet, Downie, Rowley, Pearson, Byrne

Lee Norris was again able to provide a view from down south on Mochan's revelatory performances in the Coronation Cup. "When he went north to Scotland (you can get further north than Middlesbrough), Mochan went to Celtic. And there he settled down like a duck to water," Norris wrote in *Soccer Star*. "He walked right in and banged in the goals. The Celtic fans were delighted. Middlesbrough fans surprised. And that oldie about Scottish soccer being slower can be thrown overboard. For Neil's success was against English clubs, and top English clubs too, in the Coronation Cup series. Success is smiling at the moment then on the Smiler. He is rolling his way through game after game smiling and laughing and now having another share of glory and roaring crowds. He has had such a spell before. That was in Scotland too when he was a goalscorer in Morton's side. Then Mochan was headline stuff, just as he is today. Clubs swarmed after his signature but the quiet, smiling boy stayed where he was and just didn't say one word. Finally he made that move to Middlesbrough but not before he had been the idol of Morton and Greenock on the Clyde."

Jock Stein had grasped the captain's armband for these post-season matches and would lead his Celtic side into the final against Hibernian, who had humbled Newcastle United 4-0 at Ibrox in the other last-four tie. The man who would become deified by Celtic supporters had this to say to Jim Craig when they discussed the Manchester United victory. "I had quite a good game that night. It was Jack Rowley, the centre forward, who was playing at that time and he was a prolific goal-scorer. Manchester United had already beaten Rangers in the competition and everyone felt that they were favourites for it. John Carey was the big name in their side at that time."

Celtic had failed to beat Hibernian in four league seasons leading up to this final and had been chastened by an inability to find consistency over an entire campaign since the post-war resumption of league football. Meanwhile, Hibs had won three league titles since 1947 and finished out of the top two on just one occasion in seven seasons. This was the finest Hibernian side in the club's history and 'The Famous Five' of Gordon Smith, Bobby Johnstone, Lawrie Reilly, Eddie Turnbull and Willie Ormond were the equal of any forward line in European football. A victory for Celtic in the Coronation Cup final would result in eternal veneration of this group of players who had hitherto achieved little.

The irony of Celtic and Hibernian, anything but Royal partisans, gate-crashing the monarch's showpiece final would not have been lost on the 117,060 who turned out on Wednesday 20th May 1953. Despite incessant and heavy rain the previous evening, this impressive crowd attended Hampden Park to witness what would have been considered a hugely unlikely pairing just ten days before. Charlie Tully's masterful skill would be absent from the final due to leg and back injuries and he would be a massive loss after finding form in the tournament's earlier stages. Willie Fernie took his place and was involved in the opening goal after 28 minutes; a goal that would give Celtic supporters dreams and songs to sing for generations. On the halfway line, Jock Stein made a clearance, which was deflected into the path of Mochan by Fernie. What Neilly did next has entered Celtic folklore as one of the finest goals in the club's history. "One of the best goals of my life," was how Mochan himself described the strike. "I have spent most of my time on the left side of the attack because I pack a hard shot in my left foot. Yet the goal I remember best of all was scored with the foot my friends tell me I use only for standing on. The goal against Hibs is the one I prize the most. I let fly from 30 yards with my right foot and saw the ball fly past Tommy Younger into the net. It flew into the net like a bullet and Tommy Younger took some beating from that range." When later describing the ferocious strike to Jim Craig, Neilly elaborated. "I wouldn't say any more than 35 yards," he said, referring to the distance from which he shot for goal. "You get people saying maybe 40 of 45 but that was exaggerating a wee bit. I wouldn't go any further than 35. It was a big heavy ball as well. Some players out there couldn't kick it that distance."

Jock Stein, also speaking to Craig, begged to differ. "I still think that it was 40 yards out. He says it wasn't as far as that but he hit it with his right foot. Tommy Younger was in goal that day but I'm sure the only time he saw it was coming back out of the net.

"Hibs had a tremendous side at that time. When you look back at the five forwards that they had, the Famous Five, they were well named. But we had played well in the competition and I don't think that we were worried too much about them. John McPhail was a revelation for us. He played midfield and he just played as a free player like Jim Baxter. He didn't worry about picking up any players. He was the playmaker really. Bobby Johnstone played well because he was against John McPhail and he got a bit of room to play. I think an outstanding thing for us was John Bonnar's display in goals. He had some unbelievable close saves. John wasn't a great goalkeeper off his goal line and I had charge of anything that came across. I played particularly well myself against Lawrie Reilly that night. It was a big job for us because the Hibs were a good side and had played well right through and on the night lots of people say that we were lucky. Hibs played well and John Bonnar saved us but that's what he was there for. Celtic played good open football that night and the whole team played well. In the end we ran out good winners."

Bonnar's performance in goal for Celtic was undoubtedly the finest of his career and it arrived at a time when he was not an automatic choice for the club. George Hunter played more league games than him the previous season but would find it difficult to displace Bonnar on this form. Yet such was Celtic's need for a consistent goalkeeper that they had made an offer for Neilly Mochan's former Morton team-mate, Scottish internationalist Jimmy Cowan, just prior to the Coronation Cup kicking off.

Although Celtic had the majority of play in the first half, Hibs produced wave upon wave of attack in the second period. The new-found spirit within this Celtic side was something to behold and, inspired by a series of acrobatic saves from Bonnar to deny Johnstone, Turnbull and Buchanan, Jimmy Walsh scored Celtic's second with just three minutes left to play. His team-mates to a man rushed to congratulate Bonnar at the final whistle and Celtic, somewhat astonishingly, had won the best-of-British Coronation Cup.

Celtic: Bonnar; Haughney, Rollo; Evans, Stein, McPhail; Collins, Walsh, Mochan, Peacock, Fernie
Hibernian: Younger; Govan, Paterson; Buchanan, Howie, Combe; Smith, Johnstone, Reilly, Turnbull, Ormond

The 117,060 crowd recorded at Hampden Park for this unique final did not include 6,000 supporters who were locked out after police ordered that the gates be closed 20 minutes before kick-off. Thousands of fans were still outside the ground 45 minutes after the final whistle chanting, "We want Celtic!" They were finally satisfied when their team reappeared, holding the Coronation Cup aloft from the roof of their team bus.

Neilly Mochan's first four matches for Celtic had garnered four goals. All these performances had been at Hampden Park and he had two winner's medals without having played at Parkhead as a Celtic player. It had been an incredible introduction for a player fulfilling his lifelong dream in the green-and-white hoops. Neilly had made an immediate galvanising impact on this Celtic team and had lifted his team-mates to an elevated level of performance. Smiler Mochan waved to the Celtic supporters from the club coach as the team paraded a trophy symbolic of their capabilities. The Coronation Cup proved that no team in Britain could conquer Celtic on their day and it also marked the beginning of Mochan's 40-year love affair with the club's support.

"It's difficult to make comparisons between English and Scottish football," Neilly explained at the time in *Charles Buchan's Football Monthly.*

"The big difference in Scotland is the atmosphere that the big crowds provide for all Celtic matches. I am one of the comparatively few Scots who have forsaken English League soccer and gone home to reach the top grade again. And I can say, now I am back with Celtic, that I have no regrets about leaving behind the big-time glamour of the south which so many of my countrymen think exists. Many great Scottish players have found fame and fortune in England of course but I prefer Scottish soccer."

With Neilly Mochan now scoring goals for the unofficial champions of Britain, Lee Norris of *Soccer Star* displayed more than a hint of haughtiness, as he assessed the forward's prospects. "There is perhaps no finer sight than a Mochan cannonball streaking into the rigging of the net. No finer sight than its reaction on Mochan. His joy is infectious, it goes trickling through the players, is caught up by the schoolboys, passed on by the girls, and is strenuously and manfully bawled back to the field by the men in the crowd. I don't doubt that history will not reserve more than five or six lines on Mochan. It will note that he played for Morton, Middlesbrough and Celtic, that he scored so many goals and that his best performance was how many against heaven only knows but it won't tell the tale of the tremendous career switch-back that Mochan has ridden. He fell off once. He is back on it again and, at the moment, he is on the upward slope too."

History was to reserve far more than five or six lines for Neilly Mochan, and his achievements in the game over a 50-year career would be breathtaking. Other than a Scottish B Division title, the Coronation Cup trophy, a miniature of which was presented to each of its winners, was the first honour of what was to be a remarkable football journey.

"I think the important thing for us as a club and as players was that the club had played in many of these competitions," Jock Stein told Jim Craig. "There was a Victory Cup, an Exhibition Cup in 1938 and then came this Coronation Cup. Each time a cup was put up for competition Celtic had won it." The Coronation Cup would become a permanent fixture at Celtic Park. It was a one-off, just like Neilly, and such was the striker's contribution to this unlikely achievement that Stein forever referred to it as 'The Mochan Cup'.

CHAPTER 6:

RALLY ROUND THE CELTIC

"I was back on top form and I eagerly awaited the start of the 1953-54 campaign. What a season it turned out to be." - Neilly Mochan

The Coronation Cup victory propelled Celtic towards their finest season in 40 years. In Jock Stein, they now had a leader on the pitch who could galvanise and inspire his team-mates to achieve standards far beyond their previously underwhelming levels. An ordinary player he may have been, but the rugged Stein's dogged determination to succeed, augmented by the exciting arrival of Smiler Mochan, ensured that 1954 was to finally be Celtic's year.

Neilly hit his peak with 25 goals in 33 games as Jimmy McGrory's men stormed to a league and Scottish Cup double. Yet the campaign began dreadfully with Celtic finishing bottom of their League Cup section after four defeats. Rangers also destroyed them 4-0 in the Glasgow Cup and the first league match away to Hamilton resulted in a 2-0 reverse. Neilly had been dropped for the home League Cup victory against Airdrie and did not win back his jersey until a Bobby Collins hat-trick secured victory over Aberdeen in the fourth league match of the season.

Had the hero of the Coronation Cup success gone off the boil or were non-football reasons behind Bob Kelly's decision to drop his big-money signing and new favourite of the Celtic support?

"If Mrs Mochan had listened to her husband's goal in the Coronation Cup final then she would have been breaking the law," was the announcement at Falkirk Sheriff Court as Neilly was fined a minimal amount for operating a wireless radio without a licence in 1954. As nondescript an offence as it seemed, such indiscretions were deplored by Celtic's chairman, and players were often punished or sold if they failed to toe his much-maligned party line.

Kelly demanded a standard of behaviour from the club's representatives that was in keeping with his wholesome vision of Celtic Football Club. Any acts falling below the threshold set by lawful authority would be met with scorn. This minor and unfortunate misdemeanour on Mochan's part made *The Falkirk Herald* and was therefore seen as bringing his club's name into disrepute. There would be numerous bizarre and inexplicable team selections made by the then regime over the next decade that would add to the growing rift between the Celtic board and the club's support. Perhaps as a result of his early breach of discipline, a handful would involve the omission of Neilly from crunch matches when fully fit.

By the turn of the year and in time for the then traditional N'erday derby, Neilly was back in favour, with seven strikes in 12 appearances. An optimistic *Glasgow Herald* reporter described the scenes on the terracing during Celtic's 1-0 victory. "No flags or banners were seen and there was no sign of misconduct. It is to be hoped that the days of crowd disorder are over once and for all." Mochan netted the decisive goal after an hour as Celtic finally broke down a resolute Rangers defence and the team began to claw back Queen of the South's five-point lead at the Scottish League Division A summit. "Immeasurably superior at inside-forward," was how *The Glasgow Herald* described Bobby Collins, "with his ability to spread play and Fernie of the immaculate ball control were a splendid combination. And enjoying at least parity at wing-half, the unflagging energy of Evans and Peacock denoted superb physical fitness. Celtic were an attractive team."

The championship was secured at Easter Road on 17th April 1954 as Neilly scored two in a hard-fought 3-0 victory that was a far tighter contest than the scoreline suggested. Celtic had gone into the capital encounter requiring just a point to win their first league championship since 1938 and some newspapers reported an incredible crowd of 50,000 within the compact stadium. The team lined up just as they would one week later in the Scottish Cup final against Aberdeen. In just 90 seconds, a one-two between Neilly and Sean Fallon resulted in Celtic's opener. "Mochan short-crossed," reported Alan Breck, "got the return from Fallon and, from the tightest possible angle, whacked the ball into the net. It was an extraordinary goal but the power and precision of Mochan's shot were beyond praise. No ball could have been hit harder and truer."

The Glasgow Herald was particularly complimentary about Mochan's display. "Mochan, whose enterprise is one of the reasons for Celtic's success in the championship, gave them a most important lead. It was a splendid goal, shot with terrific force from near the goal-line after Fallon had back-heeled a short corner kick taken by the outside-left. Mochan must have seen little of the goal, so acute was the angle from which he shot but the hard ball driven low across goal as defenders prepare for an orthodox cross frequently succeeds through a deflection. Mochan's shot was deflected by MacFarlane and therefore carries the luck which quick thinking and action deserve."

"One of my theories paid off that day," Neilly explained in *Charles Buchan's Football Monthly*. "I have always thought that anyone with a decent shot can get good results if from reasonable range you hit the ball low into or through a packed defence. I did it that day at Easter Road from Sean Fallon's pass and I got the deflection I wanted.

"That 1953-54 team was a fine one. We had Bonnar, Haughney and Meechan in defence; Bobby Evans, Jock Stein and Bertie Peacock making up a powerful half-back trio, and the attack consisted, for the most part, of Higgins, Fernie, Fallon, Tully and myself. I was moved to the left-wing when Sean Fallon became leader (striker). Bobby Collins was on the Celtic books too but he could not win a regular place in the line-up."

Almost 130,000 spectators witnessed Celtic adding the Scottish Cup to their League Championship win to complete the double on 24th April 1954 at Hampden Park. "No club in Scotland in recent years have done more than Celtic to ensure a high standard of behaviour on the part of their players," reported *The Glasgow Herald*. "No club are offering more to the public in entertainment than Celtic because of their insistence on physical fitness and of their concentration on attacking rather than defensive football. For those reasons Celtic's 1954 successes have been thoroughly well earned and the club's reputation is at least as high as ever it has been."

The record books chronicle that Celtic's 2-1 victory over Aberdeen came virtue of a 51st minute opener through an own goal from Alec Young and a winning goal by Sean Fallon but *The Glasgow Herald* were keen to award the opener to Neilly. "I feel it is most unfair to credit the first Celtic goal to Young. When Mochan out on the right made rings round Caldwell, the Aberdeen defence must have been sure that, eager marksman as he is, Mochan would cross the ball. Mochan loves to do the unexpected however, and he suddenly shot with great power. The ball had struck Young and was in the net before anyone could counter the move."

"Neilly was a great man - a great Celt," offered Sean Fallon when speaking to his biographer, Stephen Sullivan. "He was an excellent player too; anywhere around the goal, he was very dangerous. I used to wind him up though, saying that I couldn't understand how a professional footballer could allow himself to be so one-footed. He used to go mad at me for that, but he knew it was all a bit of fun. We had some good laughs together."

"For the first time in 40 years," announced Neilly, "the Celts' brought off the great Scottish double of the League Championship and Scottish Cup. We won the League with 43 points, five more than runners-up Hearts and beat Aberdeen 2-1 in the Cup Final at Hampden. I was a particularly happy man, for I finished the season as top goalscorer.

"A boyhood dream came true for me when I joined Celtic. My greatest kick in life comes every time I take the field for my side. Of course, playing for a championship-winning club like Celtic is not all glamour and excitement. There's a lot of hard work behind the scenes. You have to live football in all your training and your play. You have to think football all the time."

Neilly's dedication had gained international attention even in his early days at Morton. His first cap did not arrive, however, until Scotland faced England in a B international on 3rd March 1954 under the floodlights at Roker Park, Sunderland. Following on from starring in Celtic's vintage double-winning campaign, he earned full honours on 19th May 1954 as he featured in a 1-1 challenge match draw with Norway in Oslo. Then, when Scotland's pool of just 12 players was announced for the World Cup finals in Switzerland, Mochan was named in the squad alongside Celtic team-mates Willie Fernie and Bobby Evans. The honour and prestige of being chosen to represent one's country at football's eminent tournament seemed to be lost on the SFA officials though, who displayed a propensity for incompetence throughout their preparations for this showpiece event.

Neilly's World Cup itinerary indicates that the Scotland party were based at the Palace Hotel in Lucern and that each player was only allowed 60 lbs in luggage. Football boots and shinguards were to be supplied by the individual players themselves. Only 12 players travelled but a further 11 seats were booked for officials and guests. The practise of international footballers being asked to provide their own training kit was not a new phenomenon for Scotland. Celtic historian Pat Woods recalled watching an international training session and described the players, decked out in the training gear of their respective club sides, looking like "liquorice allsorts". Scotland's opening match against Austria was played in Zurich on Wednesday 16th June 1954. With the Austrians 1-0 ahead, Neilly went agonisingly close to securing a draw in the last 30 seconds but he thwarted by keeper Kurt Schmied. The Celtic forward had continued where he had left off in the domestic season though, and was impressing on the world stage. "Mochan, as he had done on a previous occasion, flicked the ball through Happel's legs," reported *The Glasgow Herald*, "rounded him and then became the meat in a sandwich prepared by the centre-half and the left-back." Instead of earning a penalty for this blatant foul, Scotland were merely awarded an indirect free-kick in what was described as, "a monstrosity of a decision". The *Herald* reporter went on to describe Neilly as, "a lively and astute leader despite the fact that he was opposed by an outstandingly good and clean centre-half. He might have had three or four goals with a shade of care and luck."

Confidence was still high leading into the second match against Uruguay three days later in Basle. So much so that the Scottish press were remarkably touting their side for the quarter-finals by overcoming the world champions. What transpired was one of the worst episodes in the nation's sporting history.

"Neilly said that he touched the ball eight times in the match," remembered James Butler. "He got a touch every time he centred it. The players had been given woollen jerseys to wear in the heat and they were completely outplayed. Uruguay had a top class defender called Jose Santamaria who played with Real Madrid and he was outstanding."

"The only excuse that can be put forward in extenuation," offered *The Herald*, "is that the terrific heat of the day took heavy toll of the Scots and not of the South Americans, who obviously revelled in the conditions with which they are most familiar."

The 7-0 reverse was the heaviest defeat Scotland's national side had ever suffered, and Neilly would never wear the jersey again. The bathos of such an episode would lay heavy on the shoulders and minds of any professional footballer. Fortunately, Mochan was able to reverse that desolate emotion in a national cup final just three years later and exorcise the demons of Basle. Even at the time though, he did not seem disconsolate. In the aftermath of this humbling defeat, Neilly had been asked by *Charles Buchan's Football Monthly* whether his country would ever be able to make an impact on the world stage, and offered an upbeat response. "Properly organised and given the same facilities as other countries, Scotland would certainly become a real force in the tournament. When you think of the Anglo stars playing with the top teams in England together with the first class players in Scotland we should be able to make a real challenge for the trophy." Judging by this particular axiom, nothing was impossible in the mind of Neilly Mochan.

The three Celtic players who had been chosen to wear those heavy Scotland jerseys were not the only members of Jimmy McGrory's side to learn from the finals. Bob Kelly had surprised the double-winning squad by rewarding their exploits with a trip to the tournament. The beaten finalists, Hungary, caught the eye of captain Jock Stein as he studiously observed their every whim. Three years before hanging up his boots, big Jock was already mapping out his dogma.

The success of the double-winning season could not be replicated by Celtic the following year. Despite building up a greater points total than they had amassed during the championship-winning campaign, McGrory's men were knocked off their perch by Aberdeen. By the turn of the year Neilly was out of the side and it was reported that Kilmarnock were keen to sign him. Having fought his way back into the first-team, Neilly was unceremoniously dropped again for the Scottish Cup semi-final replay against Division B Airdrie and missed out on both matches of the replayed final as Celtic lost their crown to Clyde. It was a hugely disappointing season for Neilly, as Kelly's tinkering restricted him to only 24 appearances, resulting in a correspondingly modest goal tally of ten. But the striker had iron in his blood and would not allow this setback to suppurate to the detriment of his attitude or application. He was always on the look-out to support new talent making their way in the game, even if these young upstarts were aiming to force him out of the first-team.

"I signed for Jimmy McGrory in 1955," recalled Bertie Auld. "The reserve team coach at that time was a guy called George Paterson and he wore the dark Simpson sports jacket and carried a paper under his arm. Jimmy McStay also used to come up to training and he was always immaculate with the soft hats and lovely collar and tie. None of them ever put on a tracksuit. McStay and McGrory were legendary figures of the club but it was Neilly Mochan who took me under his wing. I had been sacked as an apprentice joiner and went full-time with Celtic and all of a sudden Neilly told me I was to train with him. Although I knew who the first team were I had never been in their company but Neilly made me feel part of it. A big part of his influence on me was that he was always available if you needed to talk to him. He was a big one for telling you about the history of the club and I think his whole family were Celtic daft. Neilly always spoke about the young players that were coming through. He took a big interest in them and helped them whenever he could. I owe an awful lot of what I achieved in my career to him. I was very fortunate because he must have liked me. When you look through the history of Celtic, other than Jimmy McGrory, I don't think anyone had a better career than Neilly. He was such an influential part of every post-war Celtic triumph."

"I remember talking to Bertie," explained James Butler. "We were chatting about Neilly and he said something to me that I will never forget. 'Your uncle was a beautiful man.' It was such an unheard of comment, for a man to describe another man in such a poignant way, and it really struck a chord with me. It was clear that Neilly made a lasting impact on Bertie."

Another disappointing season was endured by Celtic in 1955-56 and they had only the Glasgow Cup to console themselves with. The 5-3 victory over Rangers after a replay was the club's first success in that tournament since 1948, and Neilly played in all four matches of the run. His record of four goals included a hat-trick in a 4-0 win against Clyde on 23rd August 1955. This form carried on throughout the season for Neilly, who was again a first-team regular. With 20 goals from 41 appearances in the league, League Cup and Scottish Cup, he was again the club's top scorer. Still, however, that lofty status did not prevent him from being dropped for particularly important matches. The most blatant example of this nonsensical approach came in the Scottish Cup semi-final against Clyde on 24th March 1956, much to the bemusement of the Celtic support and Neilly himself. Nonetheless, Celtic won the match 2-1 and the Clyde goalscorer was 28-year-old striker Billy McPhail, younger brother of ex-Celt John. The former would sign for Celtic six weeks later for £2,500.

Mochan was a clean-living family man. He was virtually teetotal and refused to spend his time in boozers and other less salubrious establishments around Glasgow and beyond. It had been the Smiler from Carron who rejuvenated Celtic's fortunes upon signing in 1953, and the club had won a league and Scottish Cup double as well as the Coronation Cup since his arrival. In terms of his first three seasons at the club, the fitness fanatic had played in 98 League, League Cup and Scottish Cup matches and scored an outstanding 55 goals, making him the top goalscorer in two of his three campaigns. When Glasgow Cup, Charities Cup and Coronation Cup games are taken into account, his record was 64 in his first 111 games for Celtic, and he had undoubtedly repaid back every penny of his £8,000 transfer fee. So why was he frequently punished by being dropped for important fixtures? It seems absurd that the one blot in Neilly's copy book - his failure to obtain a radio licence - could result in such damaging decisions. Yet his family believe to this day that the obstinate Bob Kelly used this as his only means of attack on one of the club's star players.

By the time Neilly regained his place in the starting line-up for the Scottish Cup final against Hearts, he had celebrated the arrival of second child, Anne, who was born on 3rd March 1956. As his young family grew, so too did the discontent among the Celtic support, who were continually puzzled at the unnecessary tinkering of their team's line-up. Bobby Collins fell victim to the chronic and debilitating trend of unsettling the side when he was left out of the final, which was lost for the second year running. Hearts deservingly won 3-1 and the long-suffering Celtic fans trooped away from Hampden lamenting yet another self-inflicted blow.

One memorable moment for Mochan during a disappointing season for the side came on 3rd December 1955 against Stirling Albion, when he scored a goal that he ranked in his top four of all time. "Those who saw a famous Mochan goal at Annfield, Stirling, can argue with some justification that never has a shot been harder or more accurately struck than Neilly's was on that occasion," asserted *The Celtic View* over ten years later. "Stirling

Albion had conceded a free kick several yards outside of their penalty area and to the right of it on the uphill part of the ground. The Stirling men noted Mochan racing over to take the kick and they could not possibly have forgotten his reputation as a kicker of a dead ball. They could have been pardoned for not making a serious attempt to line up in a barrier to block the shot. Apparently they were prepared to let their keeper cope with it. But the goalie did not even get a hand to the blockbuster that crashed across his visions and thudded into the net at the junction of post and crossbar."

"In those days, the big hitters were Don Emery at Aberdeen, Charlie Fleming of East Fife, and Neilly," reckoned Denis Mochan. "Bill Brown, who played in goals for Dundee, Spurs and Scotland once said, 'It's bad enough losing goals but if you don't see them going past you what can you do?' Neilly had a ferocious strike."

"The goal he scored at Stirling Albion," continued James Butler, "was one of his greatest strikes. I went to that game with my grandparents. When Neilly struck that ball it hit one of the Stirling players in the face before it went in and it knocked the boy flat out. He was unconscious." After the match, Neilly's mother was so concerned for the Stirling Albion player who tried to block Neilly's cannonball shot that she gave her son a telling off for hitting him with the ball. But while Neilly was knocking someone out on the park, his father was doing likewise on the terracing. "Somebody in the crowd said something that upset my grandfather that day," recalled Butler, "and he reacted and punched him and put him on the deck as well."

From a young age, Butler travelled the length and breadth of the country to watch his uncle with pride. "We used to go through to the games on the Celtic St Mungo's bus that left from Falkirk," he reminisced. "We picked a supporter called Paddy Garner up in Camelon. Paddy used to go around the clubs singing and he wrote a song called '*Rally round the Celtic.*' We used to sing his song on the bus on our way into Celtic Park."

"To the name, to the fame;
To the pages of glorious history.
To the youth, to the health;
Of the lads who will lead us to victory.

To the cups, to the shields;
To the honours we won in the charity.
To the hearts, to the souls;
To the memories we'll never forget.

Rally round the Celtic, shout til your voice is ringing.
Rally round the good old team; the boys that wear
the white and green, God bless them.

Think of all the happy days, think of the honours won;
Celts will rise again to glory, stand behind them everyone."

Like Neilly's uncaptured goal against Stirling Albion, the Camelon Celtic song was lost to the depths of time. After two seasons without a trophy, the double-winning side of 1953-54 was threatening to go the same way.

The 1956-57 season yielded a fifth-placed finish in the league as Neilly played another 43 games throughout over the course of the campaign. His 15 goals again made him Celtic's top goalscorer, an honour he had earned in all but one of his four seasons with the club. The Bhoys' Scottish Cup journey ended at the semi-final stage, though, after Kilmarnock won 3-1 in a replay. This came after a memorable battle against Rangers in the sixth round which also went to a replay after a 4-4 draw at Celtic Park. "It was not only in the matter of the skills of the game that Celtic were superior," noted *The Glasgow Herald*. "There must be unstinted praise for a side who suffered so long as they did from tactics that at best can be described as deplorable. Indeed I would go so far as to say that Celtic's greatest triumph yesterday was their immeasurable superiority in behaviour. Almost from the start several Rangers players indulged in coarse tackling; even after Simpson had his name taken in the twenty-eighth minute there was no improvement. The Celtic player who suffered the worst treatment was Fernie, the outstanding ball player on the field. He was body checked, back-charged and tripped around a dozen times. It was little wonder that in the second half he was hardly able to stand."

Rangers would go on to win their second league championship in a row, but Celtic had proved that they were able to prevail against the strong-arm tactics of Scott Symon's men as they knocked them out of the cup. Celtic had a more refined approach to the game and possessed attractive ball players who excited and entertained the crowd. This approach was to bear fruit eight months later in emphatic fashion during the following season's League Cup final between the sides.

Neilly wrapped up a 2-0 victory at Ibrox after John Higgins had opened the scoring in 15 minutes. "Ten minutes from half-time," described *The Glasgow Herald*, "Collins chipped the ball shrewdly to Mochan, who from the edge of the penalty area swung his famous left foot and sent the ball screeching under the crossbar."

The League Cup campaign also included a win against Rangers in the sectional matches and, having progressed beyond Dunfermline and Clyde in the quarters and semi-finals, Celtic faced Partick Thistle in the final. After a scoreless stalemate, the replay took place at Hampden Park on 31st October 1956 and it was Charlie Tully who ran the show to inspire Celtic to their first League Cup win. Having opened the scoring after four minutes of the second half, Billy McPhail scored a memorable second just three minutes later and Tully was the architect. "The cheering mingled with relief from the Celtic following among the 31,000 crowd had barely died when Tully emphasised his incomparable ability to weigh up a situation," reported *The Glasgow Herald*. "Kerr hit a clearance too square into the Celtic half and Tully, cutting in from the touchline, deceived his immediate opponents by going through the motions of breasting the ball but instead clipping it forward with his head and spurting deep into Thistle's half; as Mochan raced across field for the wide open spaces ahead of Tully the latter directed the ball into his tracks. Mochan survived Gibb's belated tackle near the corner flag and squared the pass to McPhail who, isolated from everyone but Ledgerwood, completed the movement as cleanly and cleverly as it had started."

Bobby Collins secured the 3-0 scoreline on the hour mark and Celtic won their fourth major honour of the '50s. Neilly had played his part in every one of these occasions and, with the rest of the squad, was able to enjoy the end-of-season tour of America. Eight matches were played and Neilly continued his impressive goalscoring record by netting no fewer than 10 times. These included scoring all four in a 4-0 defeat of Philadelphia Uhrik Truckers and hitting braces against Tottenham Hotspur, a San Francisco XI and Hapoel Tel Aviv.

Returning on their transatlantic flight from the States, Celtic's players would have been encouraged by their League Cup success, but conscious of the difficulties that awaited without their inspirational captain. Jock Stein had finally retired from the game on 29th January 1957 after longstanding ankle problems. He was given a low-key coaching role with the reserve team, where he was able to implement the wealth of ideas and methods he had been devising for years as one of the game's most astute and aspiring students. Celtic gave Stein the opportunity to develop away from the spotlight and would have the option of drafting him into first-team affairs if his concepts came to fruition. Within months, his reserves were better organised that the first XI, and the board began to ask him for advice on team and training matters. The natural progression would have been to promote this burgeoning and freethinking coach and to recognise him as Jimmy McGrory's natural successor. However those who dwelled within the Celtic Park boardroom were making a habit of ignoring such common sense options. Instead, Kelly and his colleagues set about plunging the club towards the dystopia of the early '60s lean years.

CHAPTER 7:1

"Oh, Hampden In The Sun,
Celtic 7 Rangers 1;
That was the score when it came time up,
The Timalloys had won the cup."

Never in their entire history had Celtic enjoyed a victory like the one that arrived on 19th October 1957. Only one win since then has been celebrated with such disbelief and joyous abandon, and that came ten years later on Portuguese soil. The glory of this earlier high-water mark in the club's history was witnessed in the city of Glasgow and came against the club's oldest foes.

Celtic's underperforming underdogs faced the rampant establishment behemoth of Glasgow Rangers at Hampden Park in the League Cup final of 1957. The events of that afternoon sent tremors throughout Scottish football for the next half-century and beyond.

The decadence of Rangers could not be denied. With a side to match their impressive and opulent Ibrox stadium, they were the favourites of the international selection team and had been the country's premier football force since the end of World War II, winning six of the 11 subsequent league titles. By comparison, Celtic's 'Paradise' resembled a parlour of the poor as their boundlessly parsimonious board of directors continued to hold back a side that had shown such promise in 1953-54.

Bertie Auld had broken into the Celtic first-team during the 1957-58 campaign and remained a close ally of his early mentor, Neilly Mochan. Six of Auld's eight appearances in Jimmy McGrory's side had been in the League Cup, and he had contributed well enough to be in with a serious claim for a starting berth in the final itself. When his hopes were dashed, he found comfort from the man who replaced him in the side. "Neilly approached a lot of things with a light-heartedness but when Mike Jackson, Paddy Crerand or me were out of the side, he was always there to support us. Remember the 1957 League Cup final? Who did we beat 7-1 again? I had played in the six cup matches leading up to the final and then I was dropped for the big game. It was Neilly who took my place and he was a far better player than I ever was."

The manner in which Celtic eviscerated their neighbours from Glasgow's south side had press-men in a lather. As Cyril Horne of *The Glasgow Herald* reported, "Eleven players of Celtic Football Club did more in 90 minutes at Hampden Park on Saturday for the good of football than officialdom, in whose hands the destiny of the game lies, has done in years and years. For with a display of such grandeur as has rarely graced the great vast ground they proved conclusively the value of concentration on discipline and on the arts and crafts of the game to the exclusion of the so-called power play which has indeed been a disfiguring weakness in the sport but which has frequently been accredited through the awarding of international honours to the strong men." Horne went on to praise the performance of Willie Fernie whom he believed the Scottish international selectors should have built their side around. Tellingly, of Fernie's 12 Scottish caps, only three were won after this vintage display of skill and verve.

In the opening 20 minutes of the final, Celtic hit the woodwork twice through Charlie Tully and Bobby Collins, and the *Herald* reporter rated the performance as Celtic's finest since the Coronation Cup final four years previously. The Rangers defence were in tatters and being terrorised by wave after wave of green-and-white-fused attack. As Horne wrote, "Celtic reintroduced Mochan to outside-left and that player seized his opportunity as if it were his last. His pace and penetrative dribbling and apparently new-found zest for the game had Shearer in a dreadful dither almost from the first kick of the ball. So Shearer decided to test Mochan's physical strength and straight away was decisively beaten in that respect too. Thereafter, McColl was so busily engaged as an extra right-back that great gaps appeared on that side of the field."

Bobby Shearer was a solid defender who earned the moniker of 'Captain Cutlass' on account of his fierce physical reputation. He was the self-styled hard-man of this Rangers team and his cup final role was to snuff out the threat posed by Mochan. One aspect of the Celtic outside-left's game however was his fearless nature and titanic strength, and Shearer was sorely defeated throughout this combative encounter. "Neilly was a really sturdy guy," pointed out James Butler. "His legs were colossal and he was always really strong. He got that from his father and he would normally lose about half-a-stone during the close season when he lost muscle."

"I see Tully running down the line;
He slips the ball past Valentine.
It's nodded down by 'Teazy Weazy,'

And Sammy Wilson makes it look so easy."

It took Sammy Wilson 23 pulsating minutes to open the scoring for Celtic when McPhail headed on to the inside-left, who volleyed beyond George Niven from 12 yards. The crossbar was struck again before a second goal was scored, and it was the man for the big occasion who converted it to double Celtic's lead.

The *Sunday Mail* claimed that Rangers "were lucky not to lose ten," such was their opponents' superiority. As Rex Kingsley wrote, "It was as difficult to pick out a star Celt as to pick out a star Ranger - Celts had 11, Rangers none. This was the most disgraceful exhibition I have seen from a Rangers team, especially one playing as league champions and carrying our hopes in the European Cup. Rangers' defence had a gaping hole down the middle wide enough to take the Guards' massed bands. Don't blame Celtic for piling it on, they simply couldn't help themselves. Eventually it became monotonous. Celtic could do it solo, duet or trio or indeed quintet if they felt like it."

"I see Mochan beating Shearer;
The League Cup is coming nearer.
He slams in an impossible shot,
The Rangers team has had their lot."

"Neilly scored the second goal when he cut in from the byline," recalled John Fallon. "The full-back came to close him down and the goalkeeper was almost at the near post but Neilly still put the ball in the net. He just hit it with such speed. They used to call him 'The Cannonball' as well in the early days and some of the goals he scored were unbelievable.

"The 7-1 game was the coming of that Celtic team. They were nearly relegated in 1948 and then, when they entered the '50s, they won the Scottish Cup in 1951. John McPhail had been one of the early '50s heroes and then Neilly arrived in 1953. That was a real turning point for Celtic because they started to win some trophies up until 1957. Unfortunately, after that victory there was another lull until my team came along. I watched Celtic as a fan in 1957 and always looked to Neilly, Billy McPhail, Charlie Tully, Bobby Evans and Bertie Peacock as being the main men. They were my heroes of that side."

"Over comes a very high ball;
Up goes McPhail above them all.
The ball and Billy's head have met.
A lovely sight, the ball is in the net."

Eight minutes after the restart and Jimmy McGrory's men went 3-0 up after an energetic display of dribbling took Willie Fernie half the length of the field before he played in Bobby Collins. The cross from 'The Wee Barra' met McPhail's head and Rangers were dead and buried, despite pulling back a consolation six minutes later through Billy Simpson.

"Willie Fernie had a great game that day," remembered the late Sean Fallon. "He had brilliant skill on the ball and you couldn't get it off him, even in training. Charlie Tully was outstanding too. We had brought Billy McPhail in from Clyde and he scored a hat-trick."

"Young Sam Wilson has them rocked.
But unluckily his shot was blocked.
Then Big Bill with a lovely lob,
Makes it look such an easy job."

In 69 minutes, McPhail got his second and Celtic's fourth after a Mochan corner was headed goalwards by Wilson. The header was blocked and McPhail fired high into Niven's net.

"That must be amongst the best games I was ever involved in because we were an ageing side in 1957," continued Sean Fallon. "I was 35 at that time and some of the others were getting on too. No-one would ever think that we were good enough to beat Rangers 7-1 but we went out to play football with the cheers of the Celtic support ringing in our ears."

"Now here is Mochan on the ball;
He runs around poor Ian McColl.
Wee George Niven takes a daring dive,
But Smiler Mochan makes it number five."

Having spent some of the season as a makeshift left-back, Mochan had not been as prolific as in previous campaigns. But he completed his brace by scoring his 11th goal of the term on 74 minutes. Wilson was again involved as his cross from the right deceived Niven and landed at the feet of the Carron Cannonball, who made it 5-1.

"Bobby Shearer was right-back and Eric Caldow was left-back for Rangers," explained Sean Fallon. "Normally Charlie Tully would play out on the left for us but Shearer was a hard player and Charlie wouldn't like that. Caldow was different and was a good footballer so we switched the wingers and put Neilly Mochan strength-on-strength on the left. It was a masterstroke."

"Down the middle runs Billy McPhail,
With big John Valentine on his tail.
With a shot along the ground,
The cup's at Parkhead safe and sound."

With ten minutes remaining, Dick Beattie's penetrative clearance was won by McPhail, who ran on to his own knock-on and carried the ball towards the Rangers' goal. The woebegone Gers' defence were again declared missing as the striker advanced before knocking his third past Niven from ten yards to join the select list of Celts with an Old Firm hat-trick to their name.

"We hadn't had a great year and would never have dreamt that we could beat Rangers 7-1," asserted Sean Fallon. "Rangers have been trying to get the same score against us ever since. We were delighted not only for ourselves but for the spectators because, even though we hadn't been doing well, they never deserted us. They are great supporters and those are great memories. 7-1? Jesus…"

"Here comes Fernie cool and slick;
He ambles up to take the kick.
He hits it hard and low past Niven.
The Tims are in their seventh heaven."

Fittingly, Fernie got on the score-sheet with a last-minute penalty to cap an outstanding individual display. Celtic had scripted another breathtaking chapter in their fairytale-like folklore, but instead of building on this record-breaking victory, the board inexplicably went about dismantling the side. Bobby Collins was sold to Everton and Fernie to Middlesbrough for £25,000 and £17,500 respectively the following season and the '7-1 team', who would be celebrated in story and in song for generations, was confined to history.

The drama which unfolded on that afternoon in October 1957 was, and remains, known simply as 'The 7-1 Game' or 'Hampden in the Sun'. The latter was a reference to the ditty crafted as a parody of the Harry Belafonte song, '*Island in the Sun*,' which had been a number three UK chart hit in the summer of 1957. A lover of music and dance, Neilly had himself celebrated the win by recording a song on vinyl with ex-Celt Jimmy Walsh. Using a recording booth, the two football stars belted out their version of the number one hit, '*Too Young*' by Nat King Cole. This was a song Mochan would often be heard singing along to, as James Butler reminisced. "Neilly loved music and that record was in his house for years. I always remember him singing along, '*They tried to tell us we're too young. Too young to really be in love.*' Neilly adored that song and he was also a big fan of Perry Como. Music, dancing and the dogs were always his big interests away from football."

Just six days after 'Hampden in the Sun', Neil and Mary Mochan celebrated the arrival of their third child, Frances. The momentous victory which preceded this birth even struck a chord with the newborn's elder brother John who, at just four years of age, remembered the numbers 7 and 1 being painted on a wall adjacent to the Mochan abode. Those two numbers gave cause for considerable consternation to Rangers fans long after that Camelon dyke was pulled down decades later.

Yet, from seventh heaven, Celtic Football Club went to the dogs, and six barren seasons followed their epic 1957 success. Neilly remained a faithful fixture in the Celtic side for a further three years but he also went to the dogs; albeit his was a pastime and not a descent into lacklustre underachievement. "He was amazing at the photo-finish," recalled James Butler, "He would stand on the line at the racetrack and tick-tack up to a bookmaker who he knew and then he'd send me up to bet on the winner because you could bet on the photo-finish. He could tell you the winner quicker than the photo. I remember one night at Armadale I was sent up to bet on the number five dog and when the photo developed it was the number three that had won, followed by number two. Number five had been so wide on the track that it wasn't in the photo but it had definitely won the race. They had to go with the photo, but Neilly was never wrong.

"He had dogs of his own over the years. I remember he called one of them 'Storm'. I took one of his dogs into Kilmarnock greyhound track one night and it opened at 1/3, so someone had blabbed that it was a cert. Neilly actually lifted the dog off the track that night and nearly caused a riot. Charlie Tully took him over to Ireland once to get him a dog and when Neilly brought it back he realised that it was absolutely hopeless. He never spoke to Charlie for a month after that.

"That's what Neilly did socially - he went to the dogs. He never went out drinking or anything like that and he went with people from West Carron, where he was brought up. These were boys who worked in the foundries and who he had known for years. He never mixed with the stars who would maybe go to Celtic Park.

"His father worked for Dick's Bookmakers and Neilly would wind him up on a Friday night with the coupons. If he had a good night at the dogs then he would come in and fill the coupons out. There was a £5 limit in those days so he would sign one in the name of Mary Mochan, one was Rose Butler, and he would fill them all out in different names and then he wouldn't pay on. His father would go nuts because he would have to cover it. Neilly would always pay him of course and it was just another one of his wind-ups. We had great laughs at the dogs and he always planned to have a few greyhounds of his own in the back garden in his later years. It was one of his great passions."

Following the glory of their emphatic League Cup win, Celtic endured a fruitless season in 1958-59. The aforementioned Collins and Fernie were lost to the English league, while injury permanently deprived Jimmy McGrory of Sean Fallon and Billy McPhail. As the '7-1 team' was disbanded, Jock Stein's reserves began to graduate and Celtic fans were heartened by the breakthrough of Duncan McKay, Billy McNeill, Stevie Chalmers and Pat Crerand. The team's development was hindered by a loss of vital experience though, and this resulted in a disappointing sixth-place league finish and semi-final exits from the domestic cups. Mochan missed only two matches all season but featured in the unfamiliar role of left-back for the entire campaign. His name would feature only fleetingly on the score sheet and generally from the penalty spot, although he did score a brace in the 5-0 Glasgow Charities Cup final defeat of Clyde.

Mike Jackson and John Divers broke into the first-team in 1957 and Neilly played in both of their debuts. He had also starred alongside the father of Divers when they were team-mates at Morton. Inside-right Jackson felt privileged to work under Stein in the reserves. There was little doubt, however, that the second-string were more organised that the first-team. "Jock was brilliant," recalled Jackson. "He looked after the reserves and was our first real coach. Coaching was new to us as we had all been street players before then. Under Jock, we knew exactly what we had to do and he never asked us to do anything we weren't capable of. Everyone else at the club just gave you a position to play and that was it. The whole place was a shambles apart from Jock.

"I made my debut in the 7-1 team in place of Charlie Tully in December 1957 and they played me outside-right, which showed you what they knew about football because I couldn't play there. Despite that, it was great as a youngster to play alongside Evans, Fernie, Collins and Peacock. I got into the first-team more regularly as Bobby Collins, Willie Fernie and Bobby Evans all left not long after the 7-1 game. We were asked to do too much too early because they split up the 1957 team.

"We never saw a ball from one weekend to another and Celtic were going nowhere. The place was a joke. You were told nothing and it was no wonder that they weren't winning anything. It was no secret that the chairman, Bob Kelly, picked the team. He had it in his mind that the crowd of players that I ran about with were all bad boys or something. It was Billy McNeill, Bertie Auld, Paddy Crerand, John Colrain and I, and we would get pulled in on a Monday morning by Bob Kelly, who would say, 'Somebody told me you were drunk at a dancehall on Saturday night.' We hadn't been but that was the impression he had of us and it was no coincidence that we all left apart from big Billy. We used to kid Billy on about that and ask him how on earth he made it because if Bob Kelly went off you then you weren't in the team."

The following season was to prove even worse as Celtic finished ninth in the league. The club still relied heavily on youth as another old head, Charlie Tully, left for Cork Hibs. This latest departure came almost two years to the day of the 1957 League Cup final, a triumph which now seemed like a lifetime ago. "I came to Celtic and played with the likes of Neilly, Bobby Evans and Bertie Peacock," recalled John Fallon, who made his debut during the forgettable 1959-60 campaign. "These players were already my Celtic heroes and I was a bit awestruck. I wondered how they would speak to me because I had watched all these guys as a fan. In those days, you had to knock on the door and ask for permission to get into the dressing room. It was like being at school. Even though I was maybe playing in the first-team I still had to ask to get in.

"I was classed as a first-team player but had to change in the reserves' end for training. That was the way it was back then and all these mature players were a class above. They were the prima donnas of the club. I always looked up to Neilly because I knew what he could do on the football park. I was proud to play in the same team as these men."

As with the previous season, Mochan was initially utilised at left-back and it was there that he lined up to face his brother Denis at Stark's Park on 19th September 1959. His younger sibling had been signed as a utility player by Raith Rovers' manager, Bert Herdman, from East Fife for £2,500 and had made his debut in the number 9 shirt away to Dundee the week before facing Celtic. Raith Rovers, featuring Willie McNaught, Jim Baxter and Alfie Conn, were soundly defeated as young Stevie Chalmers added two goals to Mike Jackson's first-half opener. Having played his first five matches for the Kirkcaldy side up front, Denis scored two goals before being moved to left-back himself. By the time the two Mochans faced each other again on 9th January 1960, there had been a role reversal as Neilly had been recalled to the Celtic forward line and scored the only goal in a 1-0 victory. "I had been moved to left-back and played there for the beginning of the 1959-60 season," explained Neilly at the time. "Halfway through that season, Celtic switched me up to attack once more. I have never really been a defending type but I played a few games at left-half and I think the Celtic management saw my possibilities as a full-back."

"Football is an apprenticeship," explained Denis Mochan, whose career went from strength to strength after his move to Raith Rovers. "I left the school and I played with Bellsdyke United under-17 and Carron Villa under-21. Then I played first-class Juvenile with Slamannan. That league was made up of all the good players that drank and didn't make it. I then went Junior before joining East Fife. I was 27 or 28 before I had a drink but things were different in my day. We went to training every day wearing a collar and tie."

"I remember Neilly's wages were about 12 quid a week," continued James Butler, "and he wanted two white shirts. He was always immaculately dressed and liked to wear navy blue suits. He asked his mother to get him two shirts and my grannie went and got them out of the Co-operative. Neilly's first question was, 'How much were they?' They were about 30 bob or something so he said, 'Take them back and go to Brookes.' I remember my grandfather saying, 'You should have told him they were a fiver and he would have been quite happy.' He took a real pride in his appearance and always had a smart shirt and tie on."

"I played in the same Raith Rovers team as Jim Baxter," explained Denis Mochan. "I was great friends with him and he was a very talented boy. But on the other hand, he was a lazy hound at training. He didn't want to work during the week but give him a ball and he was brilliant. I played against Neil three or four times when I played for the Rovers. When I played with Kilsyth Rangers I went to play a trial with Celtic at Queen's Park. I had been given the opportunity to sign for various senior clubs but I was waiting on Celtic and I thought I would get there someday.

"I eventually joined Nottingham Forest and then played with Colchester. Willie, who was seven years older than me, played with Falkirk, East Stirlingshire and Stenhousemuir, and he'd tell you that he was the best player of us all. My other brother John, who was a couple of years older than me, played at Junior level with Kilsyth, Camelon and Fauldhouse. As you can imagine, with the four of us playing football, there was always that question,

'Who was the best player?' Neilly would just say, 'Put your medals on the table.' You couldn't argue with his collection."

Despite Celtic having the most innovative manager in European football training their reserve side, on 13th March 1960 Stein was inexplicably allowed to leave Glasgow and join the provincial Dunfermline Athletic. The lack of ambition displayed by Bob Kelly was as predictable as the disappointment of Stein's young charges was palpable. Nonetheless, the new Dunfermline boss remained in close contact with his former team-mates on the Celtic backroom staff. "Big Jock would come through to my parent's house from Dunfermline," recalled Denis Mochan. "I would come through from Kirkcaldy with Des Fox, who played alongside me at Raith Rovers, and Neilly would be there and we'd sit for hours and talk about football."

"Big Jock would stop off at Neilly's dad's house on his way to Glasgow from Dunfermline," recalled James Butler. "Jock would get a slice of bread and jam from my grannie and he would sit and talk to my grandfather. Jock and Neilly had a very tight friendship and they stayed that way even when Jock left Celtic.

"There was always a big gathering at my grandfather's on a Saturday night as well. They would have every football and sports paper and would start discussing the games. Even though he had four sons who played football, my grandfather would never openly give them any credit. Neilly would talk about football but he wouldn't tell you anything about Celtic Park. If a story broke in the paper he would say, 'I could have told you that six weeks ago', but he never uttered a word. He kept that side of things to himself."

Despite playing 15 matches at left-back, Neilly Mochan scored an impressive 22 goals in 39 games in the league, League Cup and Scottish Cup for Celtic in his final full season with the club. The highlight undoubtedly came in the second round of the Scottish Cup, when Celtic defeated Saint Mirren 5-2 at the third time of asking on 29th February 1960 - and Mochan scored all five goals. His reward for a performance of such individual brilliance, typical of Celtic in that era, was the presentation of a box of biscuits after the game. The man who marked him in all three matches, in which Neilly scored a total of seven goals, was fellow Camelon local, Jim Tierney. "The boy Tierney at centre-half was devastated," recalled James Butler. "But Neilly softened the blow by saying to him, 'Don't worry son, I've done that to better centre-halves than you.' That was just typical Neilly."

As Mochan approached an eighth full season in his beloved green-and-white hoops, he and his wife were overjoyed with the birth of their fourth child, Mary, on 01st July 1960. At the age of 33, Mochan would have been well worth retaining if, for nothing else, to guide and assist the emerging talents of McKay, Crerand, McNeill, Clark, Gallagher, Chalmers, Auld and Hughes. But the Parkhead board rarely made inspired decisions at this juncture in Celtic's history and, on 17th November 1960, a bid of £1,500 was accepted for the man who still had plenty of fire in his boots. Mochan duly swapped Paradise for Tannadice. Neilly's separation from his one true footballing love was, however, to prove a mere interlude in the Odyssean trip that had already reserved Smiler a seat at the banquet of 1950s Celtic greats. With over a century of goals, the Coronation Cup of 1953, the League and Scottish Cup double of 1954 and the League Cups of 1956 and 1957, he had played his part in every significant post-war Celtic triumph. His intention may have conceivably been to go to grass in Scotland's lower leagues having scaled the heights of British and International football and then retire in the family home in Camelon, a couple of greyhounds in the back garden.

But the hand of fate would, of course, lead Mochan in a direction beyond his wildest dreams. For a seemingly messianic figure would return to Celtic and inspire them to greatness exceeding any comprehensible expectation. Once intoxicated by this genius, Celtic and British football would never be the same again.

CHAPTER 8:

RETURN OF THE MOCH

"Neil Mochan was very much in the twilight of his career when he joined Dundee United," wrote club historian Peter Rundo. "But for two-and-a-half years his experience was crucial in helping a fledgling First Division side come to terms with their new surroundings. The lack of a centre-forward of proven ability at the top level prompted United boss Jerry Kerr to pay a modest fee for the veteran forward.

"Introduced into the forward line beside Bert Howieson, Smiler duly obliged with two debut goals to give his new side a 2-1 lead at Tannadice, only for Kilmarnock to spoil the script by winning 4-2. But his influence was soon felt as he led the line stylishly in a 3-1 win at Pittodrie the following week when he was again on target.

"Mochan's experience and contribution of 14 goals in 23 league games was a major factor in United's top-half finish in the table after 32 years in the wilderness and his input was no less important the following season as the club slipped just one place in the league. Indeed he missed only two of the 41 games in season 1961-62 and scored 17 league and cup goals to share the honour of top marksman with Wattie Carlyle.

"Season 1962-63 was to be his last at Tannadice but it also proved to be the most successful in the club's history at the time. Even though he was used more sparingly, making 22 appearances and scoring four goals, Neilly was still an important member of the side and helped them reach the semi-final of the Scottish Cup for the first time. Indeed, the week before the match he celebrated his 36th birthday and, in what was to be one of his last appearances, United came back from 2-0 down to square the tie against Rangers at Hampden before ultimately losing 5-2.

"He was freed at the end of the season and a nice postscript to his Dundee United record of 85 appearances and 35 goals was that he went out on a winning note. In his last contribution in black-and-white (United's then colours), he scored the decisive goal with a cracking 25-yarder in the second leg of the Second XI cup final at Tynecastle to earn United a 3-2 aggregate success. It was his second medal in that competition, having played at left-back when Celtic won the trophy in 1958."

"The month after he joined Dundee United," recalled James Butler. "Neilly was back playing at Celtic Park and his sister Nan was sitting up in her usual seat in the main stand next to the likes of Jimmy Flax and a few other regulars. She heard one of the Celtic fans shouting to his team, 'Get into that orange bastard Mochan.' Well, that set Nan off and she went to town on this supporter. She shouted back at him, 'You never said that when he played for us, you clown,' and of course Jimmy Flax and all the others who sat next to Nan helped her out and backed her up."

The Celtic that Neilly left behind continued to stagnate. Two Scottish Cup finals in three seasons were lost after replays; the first to Jock Stein's rejuvenated Dunfermline and the second with a whimper to Rangers in 1963. Despite the lack of improvement, the Celtic board continued to sell as over £88,000 topped up the coffers thanks to the departures of John Colrain, Jim Conway, Bertie Auld and Paddy Crerand. As Celtic were tip-toeing out of their maiden European campaign, Jock Stein continued his managerial crusade by leading his provincial Fifers into the second round of the Fairs Cities Cup, where they were eventually beaten by the Bhoys' first-round slayers, and eventual winners, Valencia. The play-off, after an aggregate 6-6 draw, was staged in Lisbon of all places, with Bob Kelly already left to rue that fateful decision to let big Jock leave.

The early '60s saw the end of a post-war spike in attendances, and many Scottish clubs were left with no other option than to sell their top assets to balance the books. In 1962, Denis Mochan followed Jim Baxter, Willie Polland and Willie Wallace out of Kirkcaldy as he finally got his big move to Nottingham Forest for £11,500. "When I got into Forest's first-team," recalled Denis, "we were staying in a hotel in Southport as we were playing in Liverpool the next day. On the Friday night we were having a meal and then we were all going to the pictures to watch a film. Bob McKinlay, who was from Lochgelly, was the captain and he had a pint with a few of the other players. It was the night before the game and I couldn't believe what I was seeing. I told them they'd get the jail if they did anything like that in Scotland but it was the done thing down there."

Having lost some of their finest talents, Raith Rovers were unceremoniously relegated from Scotland's top league at the end of 1962-63 with a mere nine points on the board. Manager Hugh Shaw resigned and the Stark's Park board set their sights on three members of Scotland's 1954 World Cup finals' squad as his replacement. Willie Fernie and Neilly Mochan were two of the strong contenders for the job but when the announcement was made, it was Doug Cowie who landed the position. "Neilly was offered a few managerial jobs in his time," stated James Butler. "I remember Dundee United tried to convince him to take over and Falkirk asked him too, but he wasn't built to be a manager. He was much happier out of the limelight."

Linked with a move to Airdrie, Mochan decided instead to sign on a part-time basis for Raith Rovers on 29th June 1963. Cowie teamed up the ageing striker with the fresh legs of 17-year-old Jimmy Gilpin, having failed in a bid to sign the future Sir Alex Ferguson from Saint Johnstone. After 25 appearances and six goals in the 'Lang Toun', Neilly returned to his spiritual home on 10th February 1964 when he was appointed assistant coach to Sean Fallon at Celtic Park.

Mike Jackson had left Celtic Park ten months prior to Neilly's return but was able to paint a picture of the club's workings around that time. "Jimmy McGrory was a real gentleman but you never saw him," he recalled. "He sat in his office all day and never came out to the training pitch. Sean took the training and was a good man, but we were missing big Jock."

When asked how he managed to adjust from being a player to stepping in and assisting his old team-mate as trainer, Neilly was typically candid. "It wasn't all that difficult," he stated. "When I returned to Celtic Park I was teaming up again with players who had been on the playing staff with me. The fact that I played with the club was a great advantage indeed. Having gained wide experience from playing in Scotland, England and Europe, I merely supplemented all the methods I had observed with ideas of my own.

"There are no sergeant major-type methods at Celtic Park. Players appreciate there's a job to be done and, since there are no shortcuts, they all buckle down to the hard training work. When the serious work is over there's always time for a bit of light-hearted kidding and banter.

"Down through the years Celtic have always been a superbly fit side. To start with you must have players who want to work and play for the club. If a youngster wants to make the grade he must be as fit as the player he hopes to displace or replace. Training has changed and now has a variety of methods. Training nowadays is hard but it is also enjoyable and interesting. At one time it was just a hard slog that lacked the variations which exist today."

By the time of Neilly's arrival, Celtic were fighting it out with Hearts for third place in the league and had failed to progress beyond the League Cup sections. They were still in the running for three trophies, however, as Fallon and Mochan aimed to lead the side beyond Airdrie in the third round of the Scottish Cup, Slovan Bratislava in the third round of the European Cup Winners' Cup and to victory over Clyde in the Glasgow Cup final. All three ties were won, and Neilly had another Glasgow Cup winner's medal within six weeks of returning to Celtic Park by virtue of an unspectacular 2-0 victory.

Prior to the fourth round Scottish Cup tie, the Rangers players applauded their Celtic counterparts as they entered the field of play on account of their outstanding victory in the European Cup Winners' Cup tie three days earlier. Despite going down 2-0 to Scot Symon's men, Celtic still had their first European semi-final to look forward to the following month as they faced the Hungarians MTK Budapest. The 3-0 home win was as stunning as it was unlikely, as two goals from Stevie Chalmers and one from Jimmy Johnstone sent the East End of Glasgow into a frenzied state of bacchanalia. As had been de rigueur for several years, however, Celtic managed to grossly disappoint in the return leg.

"That was Bob Kelly and his stupid 'I know better' attitude," recalled John Hughes who played in both legs of the semi-final. "We were just a bunch of inexperienced boys in the early '60s and we were never told to defend a three-goal lead. Mr McGrory was a decent man but he had no tactical sense and the team wasn't very well organised. We should have been in a European final that year and it was very disappointing."

Unbelievably, Celtic crashed out of the competition after losing the second leg 4-0, and it was as clear that a complete overhaul in policy was required.

Neilly's first pre-season in a coaching role was spent in his usual manner as he chose the quietus of Buncrana for a summer break. At 37, he was still unable to resist an offer to pull on his shooting boots and appear in the All-Star Grand Charity Match at the town's Maginn Sports Park on 19th July 1964. Neilly's team, which included 10 full internationalists, were managed by the man who signed him for Middlesbrough, David Jack, and consisted of: Bert Trautman (ex-Manchester City), Sean Fallon (Celtic), Noel Cantwell (Manchester United), Willie Moir (Bolton Wanderers), Neil Franklin (Stoke City), Willie Fernie (Celtic), Eddie Crossan (Blackburn Rovers), Freddie Steele (Stoke City), Harold Hassall (Bolton Wanderers), Charlie Tully (Celtic) and Ernie Shepherd (Fulham). Their opponents were managed by Pat Sherlock and included nine internationalists: Con Martin (ex-Aston Villa), George Hardwick (Middlesbrough), Laurie Scott (Arsenal), Peter Farrell (Everton), Malcolm Allison (West Ham United), Tommy Docherty (Chelsea), Eddie Gannon (Sheffield Wednesday), Tommy Eglington (Everton), Jimmie Logie (Arsenal), John McPhail (Celtic), Len

Julians (Arsenal) and Billy Gray (Nottingham Forest).

"Neilly had a real relationship with Buncrana," explained James Butler. "He was responsible for taking a lot of those players over to Ireland for that charity match. When you consider the size of Buncrana and the fact that they were able to attract all those international players over there, it really is incredible. All they got for playing was their expenses and a shirt and tie. That shows you the class of those players.

"Eddie 'Boss' Doherty was on the committee at Buncrana Celtic and he got Neilly over to play an exhibition match for them as far back as 1954. Eddie used to tell the story that he picked him up in Derry at six o'clock and then took him for a bite to eat at Marion Park in Buncrana before heading to play the game at Clonmany at six o'clock. Back then of course the North and South of Ireland were in different time-zones. During his match for Buncrana Celtic, they won a penalty and Neilly told the goalkeeper, 'You'll get it behind you,' and he did. That was so typical of him."

British footballers often travelled to play exhibition and friendly matches in the 1950s and 1960s for their own financial benefit and many were illegal events. This makes Neilly's endeavours all the more impressive that he was able to assist in attracting 19 international players over to Ireland largely on goodwill. Holiday-making Scottish footballers had infamously played in illegal games between 1959-1961 in Lloret De Mar against teams including players from such club sides as Barcelona. In 1962 a group of Scottish professional players, including Billy McNeill and Mike Jackson, were sensationally fined by the SFA for participating in such a match on Spain's Costa Brava. The game was described by the secretary of the Catalan federation as 'without precedence in the history of Spanish football'. Alex Harley, Matt Gray, Dave Hilley (all Third Lanark) and Jim McFadzean of St Mirren also participated with the two Celtic accused in a team they named 'Third Lanark FC of the Primera Division de Escocia.' The players decked themselves out in white holiday shirts with a Scotland badge sewn on the left breast, shorts and socks and played against local sides CF Lloret and CD Blanes of Girona to crowds of 3,000. Other bizarre tales include one England-based Irish player participating in an unofficial close season match in his homeland wearing a mask to obscure his identity.

Mike Jackson's Spanish misdemeanours would do little to endear him to Bob Kelly and it wasn't long before he moved on to St Johnstone. To the eternal gratitude of every Celtic fan since the Lloret debacle, the dissonance between McNeill's behaviour and the chairman's exacting standards did not result in his removal from Celtic Park as it had done with Auld, Crerand and Jackson before him. McNeill's prowess was about to increase magnificently in 1964-65 in advance of the Celtic captain reaching the apotheosis of his career just two seasons later.

Celtic were beaten finalists in the League Cup to Rangers and languished way off the pace in the league table in the early months of 1965. It was at this overdue stage that Bob Kelly finally succumbed to an appointment which could conceivably have happened five years earlier and, on 9th March 1965, Jock Stein returned as manager of Celtic.

"Neilly always called it the 'tree trip traw,' whatever that meant," explained James Butler. "Big Jock went to Dunfermline, Hibs and then back to Celtic. Neilly went to Dundee United, Raith Rovers and then back to

Celtic. He said that's the way it was always planned, that they would both return to Celtic Park."

"Neil and Jock's relationship was always very strong," continued Denis Mochan. "They were on the same level and had a great friendship. They both liked betting on horses and dogs so they had common interests away from the game too."

The Celtic trainer's delight would have been heightened even further just five days later as fifth child, Neil, was born. As Neilly's second son entered the expanding Mochan brood, Celtic embarked on the greatest period of their history and in the space of a few short years they would metamorphosise into one of the most feared clubs in world football.

"The first game of Jock's reign was at Airdrie and I had returned from Birmingham not long before it," recalled Bertie Auld. "I was staying with my mother-in-law at the time and the game was on a Wednesday night so I told my wife that I'd sit with Neilly rather than going home before the match. We were meeting at six o'clock, so we had about three hours to kill. Neilly and I went to Ferrari's for a meal and then I asked him what we were going to do next. He said we should go over to the George Hotel across the road because it had a colour television and that was seldom seen in 1965. So we went over to watch the telly for a bit. Neilly loved his dogs and horses and he knew everything about them but he would never encourage you to get involved with the betting. We settled down in front of the television and started watching the horseracing at Ayr. One of the horses was called 'Kirriemuir' and it triggered me off. My mother had a general store and I always loved the Kirriemuir gingerbread that she sold. I told Neilly that I fancied putting a pound on the horse and that was big money in those days. He told me not to do that but if I had an interest in it then we would both put five shillings on it. Kirriemuir won at 30/1 and so you can imagine us two celebrating. I'll never forget that night - we beat Airdrie 6-0 in big Jock's first game and I scored five goals. Looking back to sitting with Neilly in the George Hotel, I think some of his luck must have rubbed off on me that day."

"Jock had us as boys and we knew what was coming as soon as he came back from Edinburgh," explained John Fallon. "We knew how we would be playing right away. In one of his first games we got slaughtered 4-2 off Hibs in a midweek game at Parkhead. We expected a real dressing down after the match but he told us that we would be playing the same way in two weeks' time. Two weeks later we went to Easter Road and demolished them 4-0. He got his system in quickly and then found the players that he wanted to play in that system."

Two of Celtic's goals in Edinburgh were scored by Bertie Auld and he followed this up with a further brace in the following match against Falkirk, despite his side going down 6-2 at Brockville. Leading up to the Scottish Cup final against Dunfermline on 24th April 1965, Bertie had notched ten goals in nine games since the return of Stein.

And what a final it was. The image of Billy McNeill rising majestically above the black-and-white jerseys before him meeting the ball mid-flight is among the most famous and evocative of Celtic's history. It also captured a moment that changed everything. The contact had been perfectly timed, the header momentous. The yellow flash of Jim Herriot's jersey fleetingly appeared in the corner of this timeless snapshot but McNeill had won the

Carron Cannonball: Neilly outside his childhood home with his parents and first-born.

All Smiles: A young Mochan in uniform for his national service.

A Family Man: Neilly married his lifelong love, Mary.

Boro Ballyhoo: A big money move to Teesside in 1951 turned sour for the tenacious striker.

Hoops are smiles better: Neilly is kitted out in his kitchen.

The Mochan Cup: Celtic's 1954 double winners.

A Football Man: Doing what he did best. Neilly in action for his beloved Celtic.

The Masterplan: Neilly maps out his tactics over tea.

A Quiet Man: Smiler relaxed at a family barbecue.

Five Star Celts: Neilly celebrates his remarkable individual goalscoring feat in 1960.

1954 World Cup: Neilly looks on at the Switzerland finals.

VME CHAMPIONNAT DU MONDE - COUPE JULES RIMET 1954

SUISSE

Légitimation - Ausweis

Joueur - Spieler

Nom: Mochan

Prénoms: N.

Pays: Ecosse

F. I. F. A.

Le Secrétaire général

Scotland's Smiler: Mochan's finals registration card.

From Paradise to Tannadice: Jimmy McGrory looks on as Neilly signs for Dundee United.

Tayside veteran: Mochan's twilight years were spent in Dundee and Kirkcaldy.

The Patron Saint of Lisbon: Neilly on tour with Bertie Auld and Tommy Gemmell.

View from the top: Neilly shared Jock Stein's vision for European domination.

Return of The Moch: Neilly returns to Celtic Park as Assistant Trainer.

Swing when you're winning: Neilly takes time out on the golf course.

Walk of Fame: Mochan and Bobby Evans walk the walk.

Right hand man: Stein trusted his Trainer implicitly.

Stairway to Paradise: Neilly heads on another European adventure with Celtic.

The Cup with the Big Ears: Neilly on route to Glasgow with Robert Kelly and Dr Fitzsimons.

Neilly relaxes on a pre-season tour with Sean Fallon and Bertie Auld.

The Winning Touch: Sunbathing with the Stevie Chalmers.

Sightseeing with Bertie Auld.

The 1950s squad prepare for a pre-season trip abroad.

Suited & Booted: Neilly at his impeccable best.

American Bhoy: The Celtic party take the States by storm.

Watch and Learn: Neilly trains the first team at Barrowfield.

Head Bhoys: Ball work with The Big Shot, Tommy Gemmell.

Kitted for Action: Neilly in his familiar training kit.

Leading the line: Fitness fanatic Neilly leads by example on a pre-season run.

All across the sands: Neilly trains the first-team at Seamill.

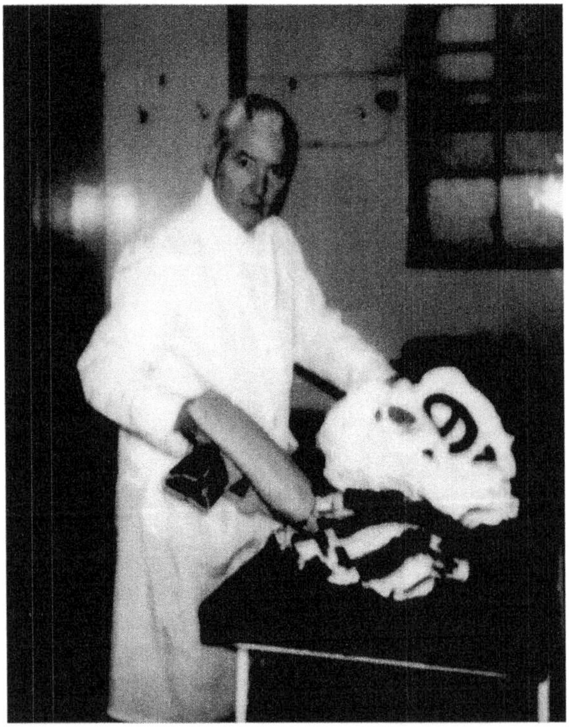

Celtic Centurion: Mochan with Celtic's centenary double-winners.

King of Kitmen: Neilly in one of his many Celtic Park roles.

battle to meet Charlie Gallagher's corner and expertly place the ball in the Dunfermline net. The Celtic captain held aloft those green and white draped arms, the same arms that would lift the most glittering prize in European football just two short years later. The cavernous Hampden Park was alive, with almost 110,000 witnesses standing shoulder-to-shoulder to share in this momentous occasion. For Celtic, things would never be the same again.

"That goal was something we did a lot in training," explained Charlie Gallagher. "Everything was worked out at Barrowfield. I hit the corner and it landed on big Billy's head. Boom. In. That was the beginning. It all started from there, thanks be to God."

Nine minutes later and Neilly's beloved Celtic would be Scottish Cup winners. The last time they achieved such a feat was in 1954, when Mochan and Sean Fallon provided the goals against Aberdeen, and Stein led the team up for the trophy. Now these three men formed the backbone of the club's management, and this trophy would be the first of many in their silverware-laden tenure. Bertie Auld had again scored a double before the skipper made it 3-2. McNeill, with his Brylcreemed-shiny hair side-combed to perfection, was the archetypal leader of Stein's burgeoning Celtic, and this honour would be his first of many.

"Even after they started winning again you never heard Neilly talking about it," pointed out Denis Mochan. "He was actually quite a shy and private type of man and he was enjoying his life away from the game by having his family with Mary."

Stein knew the value of a man like Mochan, and on 20th July 1965 promoted him from assistant trainer to trainer-coach at Celtic Park. The manager made the announcement in *The Celtic View* just prior to pre-season training and stated that Neilly would be responsible for training the squad, while Bob Rooney would deal with injured players. It was a move that was viewed as being forward-thinking, with the aim "to take Celtic back to the top as quickly as possible". Mochan, who himself had maintained a training regime throughout close seasons during his playing career, was clear in his focus on fitness. "I have always maintained that not even the most skilful man can play top grade football if he is not 100 per cent fit. A player with 50 per cent skill and 20 per cent fitness will never get the results over a period that one of 50 per cent fitness will get. Work, work, work. That must be the motto of every player at Parkhead. I hope I don't exceed my authority when I say that nobody need bother coming to Celtic Park if he is not prepared to give his all for the club.

"I can assure young players that we worked very hard in my playing days without enjoying nearly so much of the variety of training that Celtic get nowadays. But whatever the method, the object must be the same - to become as physically fit to carry out the skills of the game as is humanely possible. I am as enthusiastic for Celtic as ever I was, possibly even more so, but I am not going overboard making forecasts about what we can do. We must win the league championship, and win it more than once, before we can talk about being the great Celtic. That's not to say I don't think we can do it."

Such an emphasis was placed on the physicalities of the squad's condition that they were required to attend pre-season training on Saturday mornings. "This is something new for the club," explained Stein. "We are determined to use all the time at our disposal to get as fit as possible."

The manager realised that in order to scale the heights of the following season's European Cup Winners' Cup competition, the condition of players had to be fine-tuned before a ball was kicked. Neilly took charge of ten training sessions-a-week to get his charges, who now included the prolific striker Joe McBride, in peak condition. "It was a hard day's training but I enjoyed every minute," explained McBride after his first Barrowfield blow-out. "It was just as tough an opening day as I have ever had. Thank goodness for the voluntary training I have done at Parkhead since joining from Motherwell. Without that preparation I would really have been up against it."

"Celtic shouldn't be judged on what results we get against Scottish league opponents," proclaimed Neilly in emphatic fashion. "Not if we are to be considered a power in world football. That's what I want for Celtic - to be talked of all over the world as a great team. There is no shortcut to that kind of success." This forthright statement underlined the intent of the Celtic Park boot-room. Stein's philosophy was being suffused into his players via trusted lieutenants Mochan and Sean Fallon on the boggy Barrowfield training pitches. Incredibly, their early aspirations went way beyond mere domestic success. The blueprint had been mapped out, and Stein wanted global remuneration.

A huge loss was felt by the Mochan family during that summer of transition when, on 8th August 1965, Neilly's father sadly passed away at the age of 67. "When my grandfather died," recalled James Butler, "the family were all in the house mourning. The four daughters were in tears. Nan, who was well known around Celtic Park, was inconsolable. Then Jock Stein breezed in and asked, 'How are you doing, Nan? Are the walls of your house still papered with pound notes?' It was a tongue-in-cheek comment to lighten the mood because Nan was the banker. Jock could do that because we all had tremendous respect for him and he was so welcome in our house. It said a lot for him coming out to visit the family in our time of need but I wouldn't have expected any less because he was good friends with my grandfather as well."

For the next decade, Stein's on-pitch leader would be Billy McNeill, one of the few fabled Kelly Kids to fulfil his potential at Celtic Park. "Most of the boys who went on to play in Lisbon had come from that crop," McNeill explained. "The lovely thing about it was that big Jock started the whole thing off because he was principally involved in looking after us as youngsters. He put ideas into our heads in the late '50s and then returned to see them through. When he coached us as youngsters, he would wait at the bus stop after training with John Clark and myself. Jock didn't like waiting himself for the bus so if ours came first we weren't allowed to get on it until Jock was away. Even then we would listen to him talking about his ideas and the way he thought that football should be played. It was all part of our education. We lost a lot of good players in Jock's absence and I was on the brink of moving on as well. When Jock returned I knew that things would get a lot better."

Although there was an emphasis on conditioning, the squad were certainly not monotonously pounding the track as had been the norm at Celtic Park and most other football stadiums around the country. Stein believed in the simple art of ball practice and had championed such methods from his earliest days at Albion Rovers. "My dad played in the same team as Jock at Cliftonhill," explained Celtic youth player John Taggart. "He used to come out for training and do two laps of the park and then sit on the railings of the terracing until they brought the balls out. If they didn't bring them out then he wouldn't train."

"The biggest change when Jock Stein arrived was undoubtedly the training," asserted Ian Young. "We started doing everything with the ball and it made it so much more interesting. He talked tactics before a game and we were not used to that either because we didn't get that with Jimmy McGrory. He gave us confidence and made us play without fear."

"On a cold day," continued fringe player Sammy Henderson, "the players used to line up and Jimmy McGrory would stand there with a half-bottle of whiskey and a big spoon. Jimmy gave you a spoonful of whiskey and a pat on the back before a game."

Reserve left-back Tony Taylor recalled that players were so energised by the Stein revolution that they started to voluntarily attend sessions on a Sunday. "I can even remember Jock came out on one occasion. It was a really foul night and it was pouring with rain. Jock had his suit on and he got us all together behind the goal and he started showing us how to do some drills and his suit was caked in mud. We were all in it together and that was the kind of atmosphere that he instilled at Celtic Park."

The infliction of underachievement would not be tolerated on Stein's watch. He quickly went about stamping his authority not only through the pages of the new groundbreaking weekly newspaper, *The Celtic View*, but also in the Scottish press. "Jock knocked Rangers off their perch in terms of getting the back-page lead," asserted sportswriter Rodger Baillie. "He was wonderful at that and would phone up two or three writers and give them choice stories. His influence was such that newspapers were prepared to change pages much later than they normally would and they would get his exclusives into the final edition."

Stein's first full season in charge resulted in the first of nine league championships in-a-row. It was Celtic's first title since the manager won it as captain in 1954. The League Cup was added to the trophy cabinet for the first time since the 7-1 game and Rangers were again the runners-up, albeit having run the Bhoys closer on this occasion. The Ibrox club avenged the defeat at Hampden Park in a Scottish Cup final replay six months later to prevent a domestic treble but over the term Stein's team were unrecognisable from the carcass he inherited. Only two new faces had been introduced and Joe McBride returned 43 goals in 51 games in a vintage debut campaign. The other new signing was 22-year-old Danish goalkeeper Bent Martin, who had impressed against Celtic for AGF Aahrus in the second round of the European Cup Winners' Cup. By the time of the third round, Martin was being introduced to the Celtic support on 12th January 1966. Another unknown face was also showcased that evening in the shape of the keepie-uppie king, George Connelly.

Coming from a Celtic-supporting Fife family, the first record that Connelly ever owned was '*The Celtic Song*' by Glen Daly. The shy youngster's big brother, Joe, had bought the vinyl and it had become the soundtrack to George's earliest Celtic memories. Daly was a Glaswegian entertainer who had a number of close friends within Celtic Park. His son, Terry Dick, was taken to Parkhead religiously from a young age and eventually became a ball-boy. One match in particular from this era is vividly remembered by Terry. "I was there when George Connelly walked around the park keeping the ball up," remembered Terry. "It was before the game and I was doing the ball-boy duties so I was wearing football boots and shorts and all the kit. About an hour before kick-off, Neilly Mochan came to the ball-boys and told us that he needed someone sensible. Someone said, 'Right Terry, get your coat on' and wee Smiler gave me a fiver and told me, 'Go and get a box of lemons'. My response was, 'A box of lemons? It's seven o' clock at night.' But Neilly said to me, 'You've got to do it or there will be no game. They'll call the game off if we don't get this box of lemons, son.' So the pressure was all on me because, according to Neilly, the Russians weren't going to play without their lemons. They claimed that we had broken an agreement to provide lemons for the match. What you've got to realise was that it was the Soviet Union then and a couple of party officials always travelled with the team and they were looking for anything to complain about.

"So out I went to try and find a box of lemons. This was in the days before supermarkets and it was at seven o' clock at night. I felt that this whole game was depending on me and 64,000 Celtic supporters were pouring into the stadium from the wee tight roads. I remembered that there was a fruit shop up at Parkhead cross so I made my way up there but it was shut. I walked up to the front door and tried to look in. There was a wee wooden gap for their letters and I looked in and saw that there was a bulb on inside so I started chapping the door shouting, 'Missus, there's an emergency.' I could hear her shouting back, 'Get away, I'm trying to do my stock.' I pleaded with her, 'I'm here from Celtic and there's going to be no game.' Then I heard her asking, 'No game? Have they no ball or something?' So I explained that I needed a whole box of lemons and her face lit up. She opened the door and I got taken into the back shop and she brought out this box and opened it up. The aroma of lemons hit me and they were all individually wrapped in tissue paper. I was charged one pound seven and six and I'm walking through the Celtic crowds with this heavy box of lemons dressed in football boots and white stockings. I got into the stadium and took the lemons to Neilly and he says, 'Thank God' and he took the box off me. I handed him the change and he gave me a half crown for myself. After the game finished, we went in to tidy up the Kiev dressing room and not one lemon had even been taken out of the box. They were still sitting in their tissue papers untouched so the ball-boys all ended up throwing them at each other around the changing room and had a carry on. It had all been gamesmanship."

Another 'lemon' was to star in Celtic's next European game after progressing beyond Dynamo Kiev with a 4-1 aggregate scoreline. This time it was Bobby Lennox, who was nicknamed after the citrus fruit by his team-mates. Celtic defeated Bill Shankly's Liverpool 1-0 in the semi-final first leg at home before going down 2-0 in the Anfield return. Lennox scored an apparently legitimate goal in the final minute which would have sent Celtic through to the final on away goals only to see it controversially disallowed. "I had missed a good chance earlier on," explained Joe McBride. "Then we scored a perfectly good goal in Liverpool when I knocked the ball onto Bobby and he actually ran past me. He was definitely onside but it was chopped off. If we had got that goal we would have got to the Final and I'm sure we would have beaten Borussia Dortmund at Hampden."

The national stadium had been kind to Mochan and to Celtic, and Stein's side would have been a match for anyone in that arena. Big Jock had breathed new life into this hitherto underachieving squad and had threatened to win a European trophy at the first time of asking. Despite the disappointment, the masterplan which had been sensationally described by Neilly just the previous year was still on track. As league champions, Celtic had earned themselves a shot at the biggest prize in European football in 1966-67. The journey would take in Zurich, Nantes, Novi Sad and Prague before culminating in a visit to Lisbon. It would be there, in Portugal's national stadium that Stein's Celtic would re-write history.

CHAPTER 9:

THE CUP WITH THE BIG EARS

"I have no doubt we will win." - Neilly Mochan

"This will be a difficult match. We will be without two of our best players (Luis Suarez and Jair da Costa). We will do our best." - Helenio Herrera

"We would win even if both were present." - Neilly Mochan

These pre-match quotes were first published in Dutch daily newspaper, *De Tijd*, on 24th May 1967. The dialogue, unearthed by the eminent Celtic historian Pat Woods, shows the strength of spirit within the Hoops camp prior to their European Cup final encounter against Herrera's Internazionale Milano. Neilly Mochan was not normally an outspoken force. Indeed, he was more often likely to be self-effacing, humble and was certainly a far more diminutive media presence than his boss, Jock Stein. Yet the Celtic trainer had a fierce belief in the team's ability to overcome the 'Nerazzurri' the following day. This confidence stemmed from endless planning sessions over pots of tea in the boot room of Celtic Park and through buckets of sweat and tears on the muddy trenches of Barrowfield. He was one-third of a Celtic trinity, headed by Jock Stein, that had led the Glasgow side to the cusp of European glory. Bob Rooney, Jimmy Steele and Doctor John Fitzsimons undoubtedly had important roles in this titanic success story but, as Celtic prepared to face the Italian champions, Stein, Sean Fallon and Mochan looked every part the quintessential don, consigliere and capo of this elite stage.

"Neil Mochan is another former Celtic player who is as important a Celt now as he ever was," remarked *The Celtic View*. "For as coach at Parkhead he is fulfilling as valuable a function now as he did when he crashed in goals as a player. Neilly is one of the quiet men behind the scenes - a real backroom boy. That is to say he is much more of a listener than he is a talker. One word of Neilly's is worth half a dozen of many others'." This observation was a measure of Mochan's understated presence at Celtic Park, and the playing staff to a man respected the 1950s goalscoring icon for his hard-but-fair work ethic. Younger brother Denis is succinct in his view regarding the influence of Neilly on a group of players who were to become the most revered in the history of Scottish sport. "He was a hero to the Lisbon Lions team and he still is."

Remarkably, Ronnie Simpson was a playing contemporary of Mochan's and just three-and-a-half years his junior as he prepared for Celtic's first European Cup final. "We had a great defensive back line," remembered the late Sean Fallon. "Ronnie Simpson was something else. He told the defence, 'Don't get in my road when I'm going for a ball or you're going to get hit.' He was so important to that team and made the defenders better players than they were because he gave them something that is so important to have: confidence." Simpson had displaced Sean's namesake, John Fallon, who was the 12th man in Lisbon, but the two keepers maintained a solid friendship throughout their time together at the club.

"My first memory of Neilly Mochan was watching him in the

Coronation Cup final," recalled John Fallon. "My ticket for the centre stand at Hampden was seven shillings and six pence and I remember Neilly scoring that goal. Then I played alongside him in 1959. When he came back as the trainer, Neilly would give you a rub-down before the game. That was one of his duties with Jimmy Steele. He was also the old-fashioned sponge man. He would come on to the pitch with the cold sponge if you were injured and say to you, 'Get up, you're ok. Your leg's not broken. You can run with the other one.' When we went to Hampden, Neilly would tell you all the stories from his days as a player. His goal in the Coronation Cup final was from 20-odd yards but he had it at about 50 yards. So when we were preparing for a cup final he would tell you a tale to relax you and that was his style.

"He would come out and train with us. He could still train out at the front of the pack for a bit and then he would put Bobby Lennox out there just to sicken us all if we were lagging behind. Bobby used to just bomb around the track. Neilly would be screaming at us to keep going but he always did things in a joking way so it wasn't so bad and you accepted it off him. When Jock barked, everybody ran but you felt better with Neilly. He was a bit of a comedian and some of the things he said were unbelievable. He got everything upside down and back-to-front. He would say, 'That's an obstacle illusion' instead of 'optical illusion'.

"Then he took us for one of his famous walks the night before the European Cup final. We ended up over a mountain, over a cliff and down a hill and we didn't have a clue where we were going. There were no lights and how we all survived I will never know. He got us lost in a foreign land the night before the European Cup final, but Neilly would say, 'We got there, didn't we?' He just laughed about it."

Jim Craig was the intelligent right-back of this Lisbon side and, although he had not appeared in the first or second round matches against FC Zurich and Nantes, he had made the number 2 shorts his own by the quarter-final stage of the tournament. Celtic narrowly defeated Vojvodina of Yugoslavia before disposing of Dukla Prague to set up a mouth-watering encounter with two-time champions, Inter Milan. The man nicknamed 'Cairney' went on to play a part in two of the three goals scored in the final, having conceded the penalty converted by Sandro Mazzola after just seven minutes before atoning for his error with half-an-hour left to play. Deep inside Inter's half, the full-back calmly laid on Tommy Gemmell for a trademark thunderbolt shot to level the score. Neilly Mochan himself would have been proud of such a strike, and Jim Craig praised the role fulfilled by Celtic's coach in the boot-room dynamic. "Jock did all the talking. Neilly didn't do a great deal but, when he did feel the need to, he would do it privately. Not long after I joined Celtic I had a stupid run-in with Jock and it was because I used to wear a t-shirt under my top. I was skinny and I wore it as I would get cold at the start of the game. I was pulling it on one time and I heard Jock asking, 'What are you putting that on for?' I started to explain that I wore it under my shirt but before I could finish he shot me down, 'Not in this team you don't. Give me it.' So I had to take it off and hand it back to him. It was just a flick of managerial power because he had to show that I wouldn't be allowed to be different from anyone else in the team. I remember Neilly came over at that point and said, 'Don't worry son. It's just that he gets these odd moments now and again and this is one of them. Just let it go.' That was a sign of Jock trying to dominate and he did that on a regular basis. He demanded a master-and-servant relationship. It was the '60s - he was never going to get that. Neilly would never work that way. He would do a one-to-one with you and was very helpful to us at times. He had some good one-liners but his job was to be the sort of buffer because Sean could be difficult to understand when he was angry. Neilly was the calm head and he would go and get what you needed or give you a pat on the back and build you up that way.

"It was a strange time in many ways. At training in the morning, you got a brand new jock strap and a short-sleeved singlet. Your jersey and shorts, which were numbered, had been hanging up in the drying room from the day before. If they were covered in mud then they would have dried stiff and you would have to break them to pull them on. The socks from the day before were thrown on the table and you had to run to get a pair that were any good. I had athlete's foot three times in a year because the socks weren't washed properly and they had a cupboard full of ointment for all the player's ailments. Celtic Park was a primitive place at the time and it looked terrible as well; it was a real dark, dingy place back then.

"On the afternoon of Lisbon, I was lying in my room with Tam Gemmell," remembered Craig. "The two of us were trying to sleep because we had the big game coming up and it was taking a while for us to drop off. Then the door opened and Neilly walked in. 'You're a bloody nuisance Jim,' he said. 'Where are your boots?' I replied, 'They're over there and why am I a bloody nuisance?' So Neilly goes over to get my boots and he explained, 'We just signed a contract with Adidas and you're wearing Puma, so I've got to take your boots, find black paint and paint out that big white flash that's along the side. Then I need to find white paint and paint three white stripes down the side. You're a bloody nuisance.' I was lying in bed wondering if Inter Milan were having such problems. I remember later on during the game that I could see the white flash beginning to appear because the paint wasn't very thick. I still got the £33 fee from Adidas for wearing my own boots."

The hotshot left-back with an occasionally mercurial temperament was Tommy Gemmell. That wonderful equalising strike was his fourth of the European campaign and his 16th of this glittering season. Gemmell was the archetypal overlapping full-back who had perhaps adopted some of his offensive quirks from ex-team-mate Dunky McKay, who was often cited as Celtic's first attacking full-back. A bout of devilment a few years later whilst on a pre-season tour of America and Canada saw Gemmell unceremoniously sent home by stand-in boss Sean Fallon, and this desecration of discipline undoubtedly hampered his long-term relationship with Jock Stein. What normally fails to get a mention in the annals of history is that Tommy and his co-accused Bertie Auld, while being lambasted on the back pages of every Scottish newspaper, quietly attended the funeral of Neilly Mochan's mother upon touching down on Scottish soil. In the solemnity of the service, the Mochan family held both those players in high regard for such a selfless act of unity.

Then there was the great Bobby Murdoch. "He couldn't jump and he couldn't run, but by God could Bobby play football," said former Celtic goalkeeper Evan Williams, who continued: "I'm his number one fan. He was different class and his skill was unbelievable. He was so far ahead of everybody else." Scottish journalist Rodger Baillie did not disagree with this assertion and heaped further praise on Celtic's talismanic number 4. "Wee Jimmy was wonderful because he could produce the unexpected but over the piece I would say that Bobby Murdoch was the most influential player in that Lisbon team."

And what of the late Murdoch's vintage Lisbon performance can his younger brother and former Celtic reserve, Billy, recall? "I remember watching the game up at my mother's house with my brother James. My other brother, Mark, hitch-hiked to Lisbon. He was going in a motor with his friend and they broke down in Hamilton but they eventually got there. To get back home, Bobby's wife had to give Mark £25 on the day of the game for his fare or he would have been stranded in Portugal. I remember we were sitting in the living room when the second goal went in and James jumped up and smashed my mother's light. It was a new light as well."

Billy McNeill was "the lynchpin of the team", according to Celtic's right-back standby Ian Young. "He was the commander and everybody respected him as the captain," Young explained. George Connelly described 'Cesar' as "unbeatable in the air", and Jock Stein would later attempt to groom the classy but troubled Fifer as his leader's long-term replacement. McNeill had been Mochan's team-mate in the late 1950s and early '60s and was part of the Celtic side the day that Neilly scored all five against St Mirren on 29th February 1960. By the time Mochan returned to Celtic Park as assistant trainer four years later, the sands of time were running low on big Billy's Parkhead career. With this in mind, the memory of him holding aloft that gargantuan trophy above his head is something that every fan of this special football club should cherish; it has rightly become the defining image of Stein's glorious reign.

The whirlwind of success that swept through Celtic Park did little to fluster McNeill's defensive partner, John Clark. John Taggart was on the ground-staff as the Lisbon Lions were reaching their peak and he remembered a thriftiness in 'Luggy' that would surely endear him to erstwhile kit-man Mochan, "John Clark wouldn't wear new boots. He wore the same old things that were always needing stitched up and Neilly would send me up to the Polish cobbler on the corner of London Road. John simply wouldn't take any other boots, he just kept getting these ancient ones repaired." Clark would much later be passed the keys to Neilly Mochan's kit room and so be entrusted with the task of continuing those proud traditions against the backdrop of overwhelming change.

Jimmy Johnstone: the miscreant and the maestro. If Billy McNeil was the commander and Murdoch the talisman, then wee Jinky was the entertainer of this eminent side. Like a bullfighter, Johnstone had the skill and slight of foot to extricate himself from dangers he himself invoked. Little can be said about the talent of Celtic's number 7 that hasn't already been sermonised at great length, but the relationship between the picaresque Johnstone and capricious Jock Stein is still a source of constant bewilderment. John Taggart recalled a typical exchange between the pair, "We used to walk up to Barrowfield in the morning. We stripped at the park and then walked along London Road with our gear on. Passers-by were used to seeing us at around quarter-to-ten in the morning and so they didn't bother us. Wee Jimmy was going through a stage when he had been late a few times and we had reached the traffic lights at Springfield Road when his big green Zephyr came winging around the corner. He was a terrible driver and only ever drove automatics. Big Jock was walking about three yards in front of me wearing this big black tracksuit as Jinky shouted out his window, 'I'll be up in a minute boss,' to which Stein shouted back at him, 'Don't f*****g bother!' Regularly determined to be unimpressed by his winger's many foibles, Jock Stein knew the value of a tuned-in Johnstone. To the eternal delight of the football world, the gaffer managed to find the frequency that transmitted a sublime symphonic display far more often than the heavy static of Jinky's darker days.

Willie Wallace, an alert and instinctive finisher, had been a team-mate of Denis Mochan's early in his career at Raith Rovers. Having originally been signed as a forward, Denis partnered the teenager up front for Bert Herdman's Kirkcaldy side before reverting to the left-back position he was to make his own. Wallace was a natural striker who went on to score 34 goals in 73 appearances for the Stark's Park club before sealing a move to Hearts. Through his association with Denis, the forward known as 'Wispy' also got to know his elder brother. "Neil Mochan was a great friend of mine long before I joined Celtic," remembered the forward, who was the Glasgow club's record signing at the time of the Lisbon showpiece. The £30,000 paid to Hearts had eclipsed the £22,500 shelled out to Motherwell 18 months previously for another outstanding marksman. The late Joe McBride spoke without rancour despite missing out on a European Cup final appearance. "I had 30-odd goals before Christmas that year and then I was injured. It is always difficult to guess but, with the way Celtic were playing, I reckon I could have scored 60 that season."

By the time that McBride's knee gave way at Pittodrie on Christmas

Eve 1966, a galactic haul of 35 goals had propelled him to the highest echelons of European football's top goalscorers. Stevie Chalmers went into the European Cup final on the same figure five months later and made his 29th European appearance in Celtic's 31st European tie. As the much-lauded West German referee, Kurt Tschenscher, blew his final whistle in Lisbon, Chalmers had increased his season's tally to 36 by scoring the most important goal in the history of Scottish football. The humble striker was an experienced head in the Lisbon camp, having made his debut on 10th March 1959 against Airdrie, a 2-1 defeat in which Neilly Mochan played left-back. "I think that there was always a good bond with our team," recalled Chalmers. "It was like playing with your friends all the time, and that came from Jock. He was such a good manager that he could pick people up even when they were off their game. He done a lot for us all. Sean Fallon and Neilly were great and they had been in the team just before I joined Celtic. It was brilliant to still have them around and Jock had them working tremendously behind-the-scenes. He was very friendly with Neilly, who was a good, decent person. I was in Neilly's room more than anybody else when we were away at Seamill because he knew I was a wee bit quieter than the rest of them. The whole team were all so together and Neilly would have a wee jag at some of them and it was all good fun. I always think back to coming up from Seamill on the bus for a big game and all the boys were singing. It was such a great feeling."

Bertie Auld was well known for singing on the eve of a big match and had been a youngster at Celtic Park when Neilly Mochan became a hero of the 7-1 game. Ten years later and he was an inspirational figure in the heart of Stein's midfield. "Neilly was the most beautiful person," recalled Bertie of his ex-team mate. "He was one of those people that you never really read much about and yet he was a big part of the management team. He was the type of person who lifted the players. He would train with us and did everything that the players would do and more. He had a heart the size of himself and that rubbed off on us.

"Whenever he did speak to you, you had to listen because he was a very special person who had done it all on the park. Neilly just loved the game so much and he loved helping to bring young players on and giving them encouragement and applause. He was that type of man. He was always approachable and he was there for you at all times during the game. If he felt that you had made a mistake once or twice he would come up and say to you one-to-one. Neilly was doing all this long before Jock was manager.

"He would talk to me about myself as an individual player and how I was performing, or not, as the case may have been. He would put his hand on my shoulder and give me advice. When we went to Ferrari's restaurant for lunch, he would come to the table, sit beside me and go through the whole game. He was very thorough in every manner but he was also the most light-hearted person. He was called Smiler for a reason and he was the type of person who never held grudges. You never heard him speaking wrongly about anyone. Neilly Mochan was such a dedicated person and was wholehearted in everything that he put his mind to. He was a big influence on me and the lifestyle I had. Football is a way of life and Neilly never stopped speaking to us about that. He would come into the changing room and make a mistake and I'm sure he did it intentionally to lighten the mood. He would say things like, 'People in glass houses shouldn't throw tomatoes,' and the boys would all start laughing at him and the nerves would disappear.

"I remember once up at Tannadice I had scored a goal and battered myself off the post in the process. Neilly came running on the park and even then he still had the pace. He had this wee bag with the sponge, the bladder full of ice and algepan. On this particular day he pulled out smelling salts, cracked them open and poured them up my nose. I think he did it on purpose because he just wanted me to get up. Muhammad Ali could have hit you on the chin and Neilly would come running on, lift you up and tell you to get on with it. That's what he was like. I remember Ian Young got a bad knock on his right leg one week and he was rolling about all over the place. Neilly ran on and got Ian's sock down and he started massaging his leg and asked, 'Here Ian, is that feeling any better?' and Ian Young replied, 'Neilly, that feels great but my other leg is in agony.'

Prior to Auld's legendary pre-match East End tribal chant in the Portuguese tunnel, Mochan had his own opportunity to pass on his beguiling offerings to this group of players who were soon to be kings. "What Neilly did before Jock came into the changing room and said his piece," Auld explained, "was to speak to us all individually. He very seldom turned around and made a speech to everyone as a group. He was more inward and he would come in and speak to everybody. We all knew that he had this tremendous passion for the Celtic and that group of players in particular because we had all come up through the stages with him being there. Every Celtic game was a cup final to Neilly and he would tell you how important it was to always win. He could tell you what it was like just a few short years before and he ingrained that winning mentality in us. He was a very special person and could lift people up. He would take the heat out of the occasion by laughing and joking with us. He knew the game and knew the situations that individuals were in before a match, and he treated us all differently. He used man-management and everybody spoke about him in glowing terms. We were a very confident team and a lot of that was down to him because he gave you a lift when you needed it. In the dressing room, Neilly Mochan was a great."

Vital as the boot-room members were to the Parkhead phenomena, it was the 11 players on that Lisbon pitch who systematically enervated their Italian opponents. They did so in a style that won neutral hearts and radiated into living rooms all over the world via transistor airwaves and television screens. The global commentariat gushed in wonderment at the other-worldly talent of Jimmy Johnstone, the commanding Billy McNeill, the sublime orchestrator of this Euro-centric masterpiece, Bobby Murdoch, and the electrifying velocity of Bobby Lennox.

"Neilly was important for us every day," recalled Lennox. "Everywhere you went, he was there and he always had a smile on his face. You never got him any different and he was just a great guy to have about the place. If anybody had a problem they would go to Neilly before they would go to the boss. Neilly was great for the club. Wee Jimmy and I used to share a room and Neilly would come in every morning and he would look at the two of us and have a wee sniff and go and open the curtains, lift the windows and walk out again. He had a couple of great lines in his time. Neilly would sing, 'My, My, My Delores,' instead of 'Delilah.' He was just a bundle of fun."

Doctor Ed Fitzsimons' father was another figure who had represented the club as a player and who went on to play an important role in Celtic's backroom team during their halcyon days of the 1960s and '70s. Fitzsimons reminisced fondly about his father's Lisbon memories, "My dad played with Celtic but he fell out with Willie Maley and he got a free transfer. He played football and practiced medicine at the same time and it was Robert Kelly who invited him back to Celtic Park as the club doctor in the late forties or early fifties. My father loved Celtic and he passed that on to me. He used to play in the bounce matches when they toured and I remember Billy McNeill saying that he once scored six goals in one of those games in Bermuda. He was a big Catholic and he would wake the players up when they were on European duty and take them to Mass. They would all go with him. Before Lisbon he got a priest up to the hotel to say Mass. I think the biggest moment for my dad was in Lisbon. The Celtic bench as I remember it was Jock, Neil Mochan sat beside Jock and my dad sat beside Neil Mochan. My dad, of course, made his appearance when he came on with three or four minutes to go to tend to Bertie Auld who had some kind of bump. My father ran on and asked, 'What's up Bertie?' and Bertie answered, 'Nothing Doc, just wasting some time.' Thanks to Bertie Auld, my dad finally got his chance to appear for Celtic in the European Cup final after all those years."

Bob Rooney, hands open wide, races on to the pitch. His bottle green tracksuit bearing the title of 'Trainer' in stitched white letters to the rear. Substitute John Fallon and masseur Jimmy Steele are just rising to their feet as Doctor Fitzsimons remains seated, arms held aloft. Neilly Mochan's spontaneous leap from the bench is as energetic as the man himself. He is roaring with delight, a beaming grin befitting his age-old moniker, 'Smiler.' Sean Fallon, suited, raises his right arm – fist clenched - to the heavens. His left arm, perhaps still affected by a broken collarbone suffered on the field of play, holds his tie. Sean's decision to play on with that injury in a 1950s encounter with Hearts went some way to earning his 'Iron Man' nickname. One figure is missing from this timeless image, as Jock Stein – wracked with emotion and nerves - had gone for a walk in the dying minutes of the Lisbon heat.

"I got a grip of that European Cup," asserted the late Sean Fallon. "It was the ultimate accolade; the result of all the hard work we had done previously. It didn't come easily or without a tremendous amount of hard work from those players. It was a great day."

Tradition is a powerful opponent and in order for Jock Stein to attain his magnum opus he had to first change Bob Kelly's Celtic culture. That meant creating a new manager and chairman symbiosis before he could obliterate the anti-football catenaccio in the sumptuous Lisbon sunshine. He achieved this with a loyal group of local players and a small collection of trusted aides behind the scenes who all shared his groundbreaking vision. The brevity of this untouchable team's existence has been the subject of continuous debate for nearly 50 years as Stein quickly disbanded the much venerated Lisbon Lions team. The next generation of players would again be spotted by Fallon, trained by Mochan and managed by Stein to ensure Celtic's domestic dominance continued into the 1970s. Yet the European Cup became the benchmark against which to gauge any future success.

Mochan had spoken of Celtic's belief that they could compete on the world stage as early as December 1965. It had always been part of the master-plan, and the aggrandisement of the 1967 side proved that Stein's boot-room team were light years ahead of their time. The supreme levels of fitness attained by the trainer's physical Barrowfield regime had been a huge factor in this historic victory and Neilly earned the right to rename the European Cup. In deference to this spectacular achievement, he would often goad future players who may have requested a tracksuit at training to stave off the cold or even a new pair of football boots as their toes were visible through their old ones. "We never needed any of that when we won the cup with the big ears son," came the quip. It was classic Mochan rhetoric.

If, in the words of Hugh McIlvanney, the Lisbon Lions were a "Glasgow and district select" then the boot-room were made up of a slightly more cosmopolitan ensemble: a trainer from Carron; an assistant manager from Sligo; and the mastermind from Burnbank. The 11 players who graced the Estadio Nacional wearing glorious green and white hoops on the sun-drenched afternoon of 25th May 1967 were undoubtedly the finest team in European football and they proved that such lofty status could be achieved in an unadulterated, entertaining fashion, with a style and class that won them legions of supporters all over the world. Their leaders - Stein, Fallon and Mochan - made up the wiliest boot-room anywhere on the continent, and each of them were presented with a winner's gong to acknowledge their roles in this historic victory.

The obverse side of the gold postage stamp medal bears the immortal words, 'Coupe Des Clubs Champions Europeens,' with the reverse inscription reading, 'Vainquer 1967.' This is a symbol of immeasurable glory; the single-most sought after prize in European football and players from just one Scottish side have ever been presented with this exquisite emblem of victory. That lionised Celtic side, as well as their boot-room team, will forever remain peerless.

CHAPTER 10:

THE PATRON SAINT OF LISBON

Looking to your left, you see that majestic leader of men, Billy McNeill. The first British footballer of all time to lift the European Cup. This is the figure who marshalled the Lisbon Lions - those *Leoes De Lisboa* - on an expedition into the unknown; a journey which transformed the ambitions and expectations of British football clubs for the next half-century and beyond. Chest out and hair combed to perfection, he is every inch the captain of this untouchable side. To your right is Bobby Lennox, the buzz bomb and scorer of hundreds of Celtic goals. A speed merchant whose tally is bettered only by the nonpareil James Edward McGrory, Lennox is the greatest Scottish goalscorer of his generation and green-and-white to his Ayrshire core. A gallery of icons, this Celtic dressing room is filled with Jinkys and Wispys and Cairneys and Cesars, and the prelude to a European encounter or Old Firm derby could create an engulfing air of tension. Many minds have been swamped, many legs weakened, in this unforgiving lair where Corinthians dwell and the deified prepare. You are deep inside the cavernous underbelly of a totem of unparalleled success, where just outside, through a narrow tunnel, awaits the raucous and demanding inhabitants of Celtic Park. This is Paradise. Precious few are able to make the short journey, where liniment and expectation fill the air, on to that hallowed turf without leaving something behind. This is the Paradise Paradox. Jock Stein has been there and stood shoulder-to-shoulder with Sean Fallon and Neilly Mochan.

These men know what it takes and have witnessed careers unravel in the minutes before a whistle is blown.

And then Jimmy Steele waltzes in.

"And now ladies and gentlemen, good evening and welcome to the world's most famous arena, Madison Square Garden in beautiful New York City, for an evening of world-class boxing. It is time for your main event of the evening: 12 rounds for the Heavyweight Championship of the world. We are joined here tonight in this magnificent arena by some of the biggest names in the world of entertainment. In the front row is the one and only Frank Sinatra and sitting next to Ol' Blue Eyes is his great friend Dean Martin. Introducing from Glasgow, Scotland, Bob Rooney, who is sitting right behind the Rat Pack and, just entering the room to take his ring-side seat, is Jock Stein, who's obviously got his hands on some comps..."

The mood lifts and the dressing room erupts into a cacophony of laughter. Above all else you hear the high-pitched and unmistakeable, "hee, hee, hee" of Smiler Mochan, who has heard Steelie's repertoire a hundred times before but will never tire of these pre-match histrionics. Jimmy Steele becomes more than a pre-match masseur, Neilly more than a trainer and kit-man, and Stein has entrusted them with these roles for that very reason. A master of many crafts, Stein could identify every nuance of a man's character and personality and weave them into the tapestry of his masterplan.

Having won all five tournaments in which they had competed the previous season, Stein's Celtic would have the opportunity to contest for the world heavyweight championship, or the World Club Championship as it was known, in 1967-68. Neilly's comments from three years previously had proven almost prophetic: *"That's what I want for Celtic – to be talked of all over the world as a great team."* Now was their chance.

In a season in which Celtic won a third consecutive league championship and the League Cup was added after an emphatic 5-3 defeat of Dundee, there were disappointing first-round exits from the Scottish and European Cups. For the first and last time, the Glasgow outfit also played for the World Club Championship and were up against Argentina's Racing Club de Avellaneda. This competition was a barometer to establish the best club side in world football by pitching the European champions against their South American counterparts. After winning 1-0 at Hampden Park in the first leg, Celtic went down 2-1 at a stadium in Buenos Aires known as '*El Cilindro*', loosely translated as 'The Cylinder'. Yet it was a metal cylinder that forced Mochan to make an appearance from the Celtic bench before a ball was kicked on account of Ronnie Simpson being felled by the missile. The source of this disgusting attack was never confirmed but it would have been a difficult feat to catapult the offending object over the perimeter fencing from the crowd. Suspicions that it had been thrown from the area between the goal and the perimeter fence were rife and numerous local photographers and ball-boys were assembled in that particular area. Images of the dazed and confused Celtic keeper show Neilly with a protective arm around the man known as 'Faither' on account of his veteran status in the changing room. Mochan, as always, was there when any of Celtic's players needed him most.

"My dad spoke about the Racing Club game and the pole that hit Ronnie," explained Dr Ed Fitzsimons. "There were allegations that Ronnie was faking it but my father observed a bloody great cut, a big hole, in the back of his head where he had been hit. He had been badly injured."

Dr Fitzsimons' father had tended to Celtic's bleeding goalie just before the second leg but Celtic decided to play on and John Fallon took over between the sticks. Before the advent of the away goals rule, Celtic went down 2-1 and a third play-off match was staged in Montevideo. Neilly's memories of Uruguay were already not altogether pleasant having been on the wrong side of that infamous 7-0 defeat to 'La Celeste' in the 1954 World Cup finals. However, the events of 5th November 1967, a day on which the beautiful game died of shame, left an even worse taste in the mouth of Celtic's trainer.

Although Neilly had returned to Celtic as assistant trainer to Sean Fallon in February 1964 and had thereafter taken over the substantive trainer's post in July 1965, he had also inherited other roles around Celtic Park. As well as helping Jimmy Steele with massaging players, Neilly was also responsible for maintaining and managing the kit and looking after the ground-staff players. The young boys with aspirations to pull on the hoops not only trained with the club but also cleaned the boots, mopped the changing rooms and swept the terraces. Two skips full of empty tins and bottles were guaranteed after a weekend match in the days when taking a carry-out into the game was the done thing. It was Neilly's ground-staff boys who had to clear up the empties from the vast concrete expanses on a Monday morning.

One of the first youngsters Neilly looked after was the prodigiously talented Fifer, George Connelly. The 18-year-old was taken to Argentina and Uruguay and looked on from the stands. "That place in Buenos Aires was a real wild house," recalled George. "It was a huge tiered arena and guns were shooting confetti off and it was absolutely fanatical. I remember seeing

Ronnie going down and we were all wondering what had happened. There had been so much carry on in Argentina I think that Celtic just wanted to come home, but we played the third game and lost it. There was no way that the referee and linesmen were going to give us anything in that match."

As the Celtic party left Uruguay the following day, Connelly stayed behind with Jimmy Johnstone to take part in a benefit game at the same venue for the Uruguayan Football Players' Corporation. While that match was taking place, the football press reacted to the shameful battle of Montevideo. "The image of the World Club Football Championship was cast in a deep shadow today," reported *The Glasgow Herald*. "After almost universal condemnation of a brawling play-off here yesterday in which Racing, of Argentina, beat Celtic 1-0 with a goal by Cardenas in 56 minutes. Such headlines in South American newspapers as 'Racing won the war' and 'A public swindle' summed up the general feeling about the brutally fought match in which six players were sent off and police were twice called into action. Celtic's chairman, Mr R Kelly, described the game afterwards as 'an ugly, brutal match containing no football.' Mr Kelly, who had laid great stress here and in Buenos Aires on the club's discipline on the field, said it was 'disgraceful that our team descended to that level to defend themselves.' Mr Stein said, 'I would not bring a team to South America again for all the money in the world.' Now the future of the World Club Championship is in doubt."

Celtic reacted to their South American debacle in the greatest possible way: the Celtic way. The following season they won the domestic treble and were defeated by a single AC Milan goal in the quarter-finals of the European Cup. Bertie Auld, by then 31, scored a goal and ran the show in the 6-2

League Cup final defeat of Hibs at the national stadium on 5th April 1969. "We thought Hampden Park was our training ground because we played there so often," said Bertie. "Every time we were there Neilly would tell us about the Coronation Cup final goal he scored against Hibs."

Bobby Lennox scored in the 4-0 annihilation of Rangers in the Scottish Cup final on 26th April 1969 and remembered George Connelly's performance that day, as the youngster progressed from Neilly's ground-staff boy to a fully-fledged first-team star. "He just took it so easily and so casually," explained Bobby. "He had great ability and was wonderful with the ball at his feet and always looked so laidback. For our third goal he just took the ball from the Rangers defender, rounded the keeper and knocked it in like he was playing a practice game up the park. Big George was so cool."

Connelly was a trailblazer for another batch of Celtic talent being produced on that seemingly endless Barrowfield conveyor belt. He would form part of a crop referred to as 'The Quality Street Gang' and by the end of the 1968-69 season the contemporaneous Lou Macari, Kenny Dalglish and Davie Hay had also made first-team appearances. "All the players would do their warm-up with Neilly at Barrowfield," recalled Hay. "Nowadays teams are into stretching first but our warm-up was a straight lap. We did what was called a raw run of 220 yards. Then the two groups would be split up and either Sean Fallon or Willie Fernie would take the younger players for shooting practice or whatever we were working on. Big Jock would be down the other end with the first-team and invariably we'd all come together and play a game. It was the first-team against the reserves and it was two-touch and Neilly would play in those games. We were playing against the best in

Europe and developed an attitude that we were able to play at the very top level of the game. We learned our trade from the greatest Celtic team ever.

"Big Jock was obviously the genius as far as football goes but Neilly and Sean always instilled in us just how important it was to play for Celtic. They made us understand what it meant to play in front of those fans and never to let them or ourselves down.

"I liked Neilly a lot but he would be quiet at times. I remember he would get the bus up with some of the younger boys before he drove and he would hardly speak. He would sit there and read his *Sporting Life* because he liked a bet."

As well as the youngsters, another new face in the Celtic Park dressing room was Tommy Callaghan, a £35,000 capture from Dunfermline. "I remember when Jock Stein was leaving Dunfermline to go to Hibs, he asked me if I wanted to go with him," recalled the record buy. "So it was great to finally rejoin him at Celtic. We used to go down to Seamill for a few days to prepare for big games and Neilly would take us for walks to get us relaxed. Big Jock believed in having us all together and the laughs we got were fantastic. On the bus up to Glasgow everyone would have a sing-song. Then we would start seeing the crowds of supporters and the excitement began to grow. Celtic Park was wonderful on European nights.

"There were certain things that went on that were unbelievable, especially when you consider that this was now a European giant of a club. If you were lying on the treatment table, Bob Rooney would come in with his white doctor's jacket on and a fag hanging out the side of his mouth. He would be checking you out and the fag ash would be falling on your injured leg."

For a spell during 1969-70, it looked as though Celtic were about to emulate their perfect year of three seasons before. The League Cup had already been secured, virtue of a 1-0 defeat of Saint Johnstone, when the Mochans were blessed with the birth of their sixth child, Clare, on 19th December 1969. Memories of the St Jakob Stadium in Basle were less than fruitful for Neilly as it was at that venue that he endured one of his worst moments as a player: the 7-0 defeat to Uruguay at the 1954 World Cup. His second visit to this arena in the first leg of the European Cup's opening round was far more satisfying. Celtic returned home with a scoreless draw and overcame the Swiss champions 2-0 in the home leg. Benfica and Fiorentina were eliminated before the 'Battle of Britain' semi-final against Leeds United, of which the first leg took place at Elland Road.

"I went down to that game with Kenny Dalglish, Davie Cattanach and Alex Smith," recalled John Gorman. "Alex drove and we were meant to be staying at Billy Bremner's house because he and Alex were best friends. When we got down there, Billy's house was all locked up and there was no sign of him so we broke in. When we went to the game that night our big pal, George Connelly, scored the goal and we were all jumping around like schoolboys. After the match we went back to Billy's house and sat up until four in the morning talking about football with Billy, Jack Charlton, Peter Lorimer and Eddie Gray. What an amazing night that was."

The disappointment of a 3-1 Scottish Cup final defeat to Aberdeen was sandwiched in between two incredible victories over the English champions. After Connelly's goal separated the sides in Leeds, Celtic won the return at Hampden Park 2-1 and set up their second European Cup final.

By the time that Celtic travelled to the San Siro to face Dutch champions Feyenoord, they had already wrapped up their fifth successive league title. "All the young players went over to Milan," explained Gorman. "When Celtic played Inter Milan in Lisbon, we were the underdogs and no-one could see beyond the Italians. The situation in 1970 was the opposite. We were the top dogs and we underestimated Feyenoord."

"That was one of the biggest mysteries of my time with Celtic," asserted John Fallon. "I don't know if big Jock thought that we just had to show up but that was the sort of impression he gave. He didn't seem too worried about them because that Feyenoord team were relatively unknown, just like the Celtic side in '67. But what a team they were and they did to us exactly what we did to Inter Milan. That was the biggest injury we ever suffered. We thought we were better than them but they gave us a right kick up the proverbial."

"We didn't play particularly well on the night and Feyenoord deserved to win the cup," considered Bobby Lennox. "But I still feel had we got to the final whistle with a draw then we could have done better in the replay. Everybody seemed to think that we were certainties but most of the guys didn't think that. We knew that no bad team gets to the European Cup final and that we had a game on our hands. We didn't think that Jock would have changed the team so quickly after that. There was a lot of experience in our team and the young boys needed that experience to help them come through. I suppose losing the final was the defining moment when he decided that he better start bringing the boys through."

Neilly's second European Cup medal was to be a loser's one but with

Celtic on an amazing run of league championship wins, it would have been a reasonable assumption to believe that there were more continental finals to look forward to in the coming seasons. Stein was placing his faith in the new crop to continue what the Lisbon Lions had started. "Neilly was always egging them on," John Fallon said of the club's emerging youngsters. "He would tell them in the practice games at training, 'These are old men now. Come on, you can beat them.' The Quality Street Kids were something to behold. They were an absolutely fantastic group of players."

The expectation was that this magnificent group of youngsters would be Celtic's driving force as they entered the 1970s. Neilly himself finally decided to enhance his own driving force in the form of a licence and vehicle, much to the amusement - and fear - of anyone who ever entered a car with him at the wheel. "He used to always travel by train as a player," recalled Denis Mochan. "When he finally got a car he was the worst driver on the road. Everyone around Falkirk used to go through the Peter Smith school of motoring and he once told me that Neilly Mochan was the worst driver he ever had. He explained that Neilly called him and asked for a few lessons because he was sitting his test the following week. The international game was at Wembley that week and, although Peter won't admit it, I bet you Neilly got him tickets and he somehow passed his test."

"He was a hopeless driver," agreed James Butler. "He told me that he stopped at Kemper Avenue in Falkirk during his test and gave the examiner two tickets for Wembley and that's how he got his driver's licence. There is no way he would have passed it otherwise."

"Him starting driving was a problem because he was the worst driver ever," remembered Bertie Auld. "He bought a car off one of the players, I'll not mention his name, but he was driving this car down Todd Street in Glasgow and the breaks wouldn't work. He was on the big hill that led to the dog track and he was trying to push his foot down on the break but the car just kept getting faster as it went down the hill. He had to keep hitting the car off the wall on the way down the road to slow it down and by the time he got into Celtic Park it was covered in dents. All the players were getting changed when Neilly walked into the dressing room and says to the boy who sold him the motor, 'You call that a car? You shouldn't have bothered putting the brakes there and just left the floor open. I could have stopped the thing quicker with my feet.' He never let the culprit forget that."

Stein's side embarked on their end-of-season trip to America with their new gang of kids in tow, including a certain Kenny Dalglish, then a promising youth with five first-team games under his belt. The future King Kenny had only fond memories of this stage in his development, and of the role played by Celtic's Smiler. "Neilly was hugely respected by all of the players," asserted Kenny. "The youngsters and the senior pros looked up to him because of the magnificent playing career that he'd had. Big Jock obviously knew him very well from their playing days and that relationship continued as part of the management team. There was no doubting who the gaffer was, but Jock had Sean and Neilly in roles that they were well suited to.

"Sean and Willie Fernie worked closely with the reserves, and Willie represented everything that Celtic Football Club stood for. He was still a fantastic footballer even at that age and was so enthusiastic at training that he made it enjoyable for all of us. He loved just getting the ball out and he really educated us. Jock was never far away even though he was looking after the first-team, but he had a great backroom team and they all worked so well together.

"Neilly was still very fit and when we went to Seamill Hydro he would lead the run in training but he was also great fun and was always on the wind-up. I remember we were all just wee boys at the time and we went away with the first-team on the pre-season tour. We were all out sunbathing and Neilly came over to see us. He told us that the suntan lotion we were using was bad for our skin and he gave us a tub of his Vaseline. We believed him and started putting the Vaseline on so we could get a good tan. We were like lobsters by the end of the day and I'm sure he would have a good laugh at us that night."

"Let's just say that Neilly offered us the Vaseline and I was slightly redder than normal," added Davie Hay. "He loved winding us up and he had this distinctive giggle. He would break into fits of laughter and that's when you knew that you'd been had. Because Neilly had been a player himself he knew that side of the game and the need for camaraderie in the dressing room. He would wind us up to keep us in our place but in a good way. He never let us get carried away with ourselves."

But it wasn't all fun and laughter for Mochan during these halcyon days. One of the most testing experiences of his life came the following season as 66 football fans died on stairway 13 at the Old Firm match at Ibrox on 2nd January 1971. "That was the one thing that really affected him," confirmed his youngest son, Neil. "He wasn't the type of person who went on about things all that often but I asked him a few times and he would shake his head and say things like, 'They were just young laddies'. It was almost as if he was thinking back to those awful scenes and a sense of sadness came over him. He was one of the people who carried bodies from the terraces and was helping to get the injured into ambulances with big Jock. It had a profound effect on him."

"My dad was the only doctor at the Ibrox disaster with any drugs," remembered Doctor Ed Fitzsimons. "I was at the game and was waiting for my dad outside the ground. All these ambulances were going in and out of the stadium and I was wondering what was going on. It was about eight o'clock at night when he finally came out of Ibrox and I had been waiting for hours. My dad was a tough man and he put his head down on the roof of the car that night and started to cry. All he would say to me was, 'They didn't have any shoes'. It was because the crowd were lifted out their shoes in the crush. There were piles and piles of shoes. My dad had one ampoule of adrenaline and he gave that shot straight into the heart of a man whom he thought may have survived. It had the electric shock type of reaction and that man came through. Rangers were always good to my dad. When he passed away there was a good representation from the club at his funeral."

Neilly had also been witness to the Shawfield disaster of 14th December 1957, when a wall collapsed during a league match between Celtic and Clyde. Supporters at the front of the terracing were crushed and a 12-year-old boy was killed with many others hospitalised. Another youngster, nine-year-old Peter Tomasso, was lifted from the wreckage to safety by Mochan, who had rushed off the park to assist. This remarkable man had witnessed the greatest highs of Celtic Football Club since the war but had also dealt with some of the most harrowing moments imaginable.

Celtic's sixth successive league championship soon arrived and was accompanied by a Scottish Cup success. Their European Cup run ended at the quarter-final stage though, where another Dutch side, this time Ajax, proved too strong. The League Cup final had been lost 1-0 to Rangers but this defeat was avenged at the same stage of the Scottish Cup, with a 2-1 win secured by goals from Lou Macari and Harry Hood. "People won't believe it," stated Macari, "but the playing side of Celtic Park was run by Jock Stein, Neilly Mochan, Sean Fallon, Willie Fernie; Bob Rooney, the physio; and Jimmy Steele, the masseur. There were lots of scouts and other people on the fringes so I don't want to be missing anybody out, but those six people more or less ran the place and, fortunately for us all, those six people guided myself, Kenny Dalglish, Danny McGrain and Davie Hay on to good careers."

Another Celtic career that looked to be destined for greatness was that of Grangemouth boy Brian McLaughlin. When Jock Stein handed the 16-year-old his debut among a hybrid side peppered with Lisbon Lions and Quality Street Kids, it was a clear indication of the player's vast potential. That first-team bow had come in the quarter-final of the 1971-72 League Cup, when Celtic trounced Clydebank 6-2 in the tie's second leg. "They used to call young Brian 'Super' because his ability was out of this world," explained James Butler. "Neilly was really fond of Super, who was a great wee guy. They were playing at Hampden and Neilly took him out on to the park before the game started. They used to take some of the young boys along for the experience so Super wouldn't have been in the playing squad at that time. He asked Brian if he had played at Hampden before and he confirmed that he had played there with Saint Mungo's school. Then Neilly asked him, 'Did you score that day?' and young Brian told him he hadn't. They were standing about 45 yards from goal and Neilly just pointed to the pitch and said, 'I scored from here, son'. That was the type of thing Neilly would do."

"Brian used to say that as a young player he would get picked up by Neilly every morning," recalled John Sludden, a great friend of the prodigious McLaughlin, whose career was irrevocably damaged by a horrendous knee injury sustained at the age of 18. "George Connelly would be sitting in the passenger's seat and Brian couldn't believe it. His favourite player was Bobby Murdoch but he also spoke very highly of big George. Neilly said to Brian one day in the car coming home that he didn't have a driver's licence and he asked Brian if he knew where he could get one. Mrs McLaughlin phoned into the stadium the next day and asked to speak to Jock Stein as she was worried that Neilly was driving her son back and forward to Glasgow with no licence. Big Jock just said to her, 'Mrs McLaughlin, that's just Neilly.'

"I went to St Mungo's High School in Falkirk and the first player that you ever heard about at school was Brian McLaughlin. The janitor was a Celtic scout called Tom Harvey and he said that Brian was the best schoolboy they had ever seen playing. We were both capped at schoolboy level and then we both signed for Celtic so I followed in his path.

"Brian rarely spoke about the tackle that caused his injury. But he did tell me once that the previous week they had played Dunfermline and Brian had knocked the ball inside and gone into a block tackle. The defender won the ball and Jock had said to him that he better watch what he was doing or he would end up getting himself injured. The following week they were playing Clyde at Celtic Park and he knocked the ball a bit too far but he could hear big Jock's words ringing in his ears. He was just trying to make sure that he didn't lose out but the defender (Clyde's Willie McVie) made that dreadful challenge and it virtually ended Brian's top-flight career.

"My uncle Neilly never spoke about what was going on inside Celtic Park; he never discussed players or anything like that. I do remember, however, that he once said to me that if you pass the ball to Brian McLaughlin then Celtic will have a chance."

The league championship was won for a seventh consecutive season in 1971-72 and the Scottish Cup retained after a 6-1 win against Hibernian. "Even then you could see that Kenny Dalglish was just that bit above the rest," asserted Pat Stanton, who captained Hibs at Hampden Park on 6th May 1972. "He was a terrific player who was very strong and very quick. He wasn't quick over thirty yards but he was over ten and that's all you need. Add that to his quick thinking and he was always a danger."

Dalglish failed to score in the emphatic Scottish Cup victory but did manage to find the net in the League Cup final, albeit in a shock 4-1 defeat to unfancied Partick Thistle. Kenny's quest for a European Cup medal was then thwarted at the semi-final stage as Inter Milan defeated their old foes on penalties. "Neilly used to do this trick with a table-tennis ball," remembered Dalglish. "He would throw the ball in the air and catch it on his forehead. Then he would walk around the changing room balancing this ball on his head. It was an incredible trick." A young Dalglish may have been duped like many others at Celtic Park for Neilly was only able to balance the ball with the aid of his trusted sticking agent, Vaseline, on his brow. "People like Neilly

Mochan are really important to clubs like Celtic," continued Kenny. "Players and managers come and go at football clubs and it is vitally important to have a figure like Neilly who knows the place inside-out."

Dalglish was able to score in two further domestic finals the following season but both resulted in defeats: to Pat Stanton's Hibernian (2-1 in the League Cup) and Rangers (3-2 Scottish Cup). Celtic did retain their league crown for the eighth consecutive year but their European Cup run lasted just two rounds after a loss to Ujpest Dosza. Andy Lynch signed for his boyhood heroes from Hearts during the 1972-73 campaign and remembered the boot-room dynamic that existed between Stein and his former team-mates. "Big Jock made all the decisions but he did rely on Sean and Neilly heavily because you can't do it all yourself," explained Lynch. "Neilly would still occasionally do some of the training by the time I signed and he would be on the bench during every game. If we had an injury, Neilly would come out with his bag and magic sponge and that was about all he had.

"I remember playing against Rangers and going into a challenge where it was obvious that the boy had gone in to hurt me. I was in agony, writhing about on the pitch and I actually thought my leg was broken. Then Neilly ran on with his wee bag and the referee was just standing there taking no action. When Neilly peeled my sock back he could see my leg was in an awful mess. There were two holes in my shin where the player's studs had got me and I still have the scar to this day. The referee, Ian Foote, was well known for not being particularly fair when refereeing matches involving Celtic and he could quite clearly see the damage the tackle had caused me. Neilly was absolutely raging as he sponged my leg. He fumed, 'What are you playing at Andy? Big

Jock told you that we'd get nothing from him. He'll give us nothing.' Neilly made out that he was angry at me but he was doing it to get his point across to this ref, knowing that he would hear every word. That was what it was like against Rangers and we all knew it."

The nine-in-a-row season again threatened a clean sweep as Stein's Celtic juggernaut showed no signs of slowing down. Both domestic cup finals were contested against Tayside teams. Dundee won the League Cup 1-0 but Neilly's ex-club United were convincingly defeated 3-0 in the Scottish Cup final to secure Celtic's 20th domestic trophy since the return of Jock Stein. Another outstanding European campaign ended at the semi-final stage after Celtic were kicked, punched, scratched and pulled out of the competition against Atletico Madrid. "That was the worst game I ever played in for violence on the park," asserted Pat McCluskey. "It was mayhem. No-one seen what really happened going up the tunnel but it was a like a bar-room brawl. I think we won the battle in the tunnel. We suffered over there though because there were death threats to wee Jimmy and we needed an armed escort to go to training."

The Atletico Madrid fiasco can be bracketed with Montevideo in terms of farce and fiasco. Celtic went down 2-0 away from home but the beautiful game had been shamed in the first leg as Celtic, and particularly Jimmy Johnstone, were literally kicked off the park. No fewer than ten Atletico players were either sent off or booked in that brutal encounter and the post-match fisticuffs in the Celtic Park tunnel even involved the mild-mannered Mochan.

Celtic's domestic dominance was curtailed the following year as, unthinkably, Rangers won the league and Hibs came second. The league table was more akin to that of Neilly's playing days 20 years previously and not until 1977 would Celtic win the championship title again. Another new crop of youth players were progressing into the first-team dressing room and Tommy Burns followed in the footsteps of George Connelly and Brian McLaughlin as one of Neilly's ground-staff boys. "I always remember when Tommy was on the ground-staff," explained Frank Welsh. "I would be heading to get my bus home and I would see Tommy struggling along the road towards Celtic Park with two bottles of Irn Bru and two fish suppers. That was Neilly Mochan and Bob Rooney sending him down to get them their dinner."

Despite losing out on the league for the first time in a decade, Celtic still won the two domestic cups and the 3-1 Scottish Cup final victory against Airdrie heralded the end of Billy McNeill's glorious Celtic career. "That game was one of the highlights of my career," said Pat McCluskey. "Big Billy had told us before the game that he was retiring afterwards, so it was good to be a part of history. Paul Wilson never scored a goal in his life with his head and somehow he scored two that day. Paul's mother had died two or three days before it and we had all gone to the funeral. Big Jock had said to Paul that he would understand if he couldn't play but he decided he was up for it. He scored two goals and that showed the strength of him."

"I remember Billy saying that he maybe felt he could have gone on for another couple of seasons," recalled Andy Lynch. "He could have played on without a doubt but at the same time he wanted to go out at the top and I think big Jock encouraged him to call it a day. Billy maybe went along with it thinking that he would get into management next. Billy's reading of the game was unbelievable. His dominance in the air had to be seen to be believed - there was no player in the British game who had the dominance of Billy McNeill. When I was at left-back, I knew he would win any balls coming into the box from corners, free-kicks or just normal play. He was unbeatable in those days and we left everything for him."

"I remember when my dad brought the Scottish Cup home with the green and white ribbons on it," explained Neil Junior. "There was a celebration in our house and then later on that evening some of the boys ended up running around the streets of Camelon carrying the Scottish Cup above their head. Not a replica, the actual trophy. It's crazy when you think about it now but it didn't seem unusual to me at the time. I had been brought up with this club as part of my daily life and when my dad went to Celtic Park he was going to his work. Jock Stein was his work-mate. I remember Jock used to phone the house and I would pick it up. He would talk to me for five or ten minutes before asking to speak to my dad but, again, that didn't seem strange to me. This was John, who was my dad's work colleague and friend. When I went to the games I would often be hanging around the reception area waiting for my dad afterwards. He would be in his boot-room and it was one of those situations where depending on who was around would determine on whether my dad and big Jock would stop talking. There were plenty of people who would walk into the boot-room and the subject of conversation would change completely. They were very tight and only a few people were in that inner circle. My dad used to give me a ball to keep me occupied and I would use some of the trophies that were lying around as goalposts. I do recall using the Coronation Cup as a goalpost when I was kicking that ball around one

Saturday afternoon but, as I said, this was all normal to me."

The mutual trust that existed between the former team-mates also ensured that, when problems did occur, Stein was quick to call on Mochan's assistance. "When wee Jinky got lifted in Hamilton and was lying in the cells, Jock Stein came out in a taxi to get Neilly" explained James Butler. "Big Jock wouldn't get out the car, he just shouted for Neilly and away they went. It was the same when Brian McLaughlin was going through some difficult times in his private life and he wasn't turning up for training. It was Neilly who had to go and try to find him, and he went to his mother's house looking for him. Big Stein had a lot of trust in Neilly and they had a very strong bond."

The 1976-77 double-winning season was sandwiched between two trophyless campaigns. Just ten years had passed since Lisbon, but the only Lion left in paradise was Bobby Lennox. The subsequent changing of the guard in 1978 was inevitable, but it left Neilly and Steelie as the only remaining members of Stein's boot-room. But while they would defiantly carry on the traditions set down by their comrade, the corridors of this dear green place would never be the same again.

Stein had created a philosophy at Celtic Park that cemented a winning mentality throughout every facet of the football club. It is this ethos – Stein's ethos - which still exists to this day. The manner in which victory is attained is often referred to as 'the Celtic way' and that seed was sown by the club's greatest manager in 1965 and cultivated until he was relieved of his duties in 1978. During that glorious period, Big Jock built teams to scale the highest peaks of European football. His ways were pioneering and he knew that, in order to implement his blueprint for success, he would require a talented and closely knit backroom team. Sean Fallon's biographer, Stephen Sullivan, realised through speaking extensively with 'The Iron Man' that the togetherness that existed between these boot-room Bhoys was a key aspect of the Stein success story. "In reflecting contentedly on the Lisbon era," wrote Stephen, "Sean might have been seen to be stating the obvious when he told me, 'We really did have a great team'. Yet the team he was enthusing about consisted not of 11 men on the park, but of a handful on the bench. And the assessment was every bit as valid.

"Through my conversations with Sean, it became quickly and abundantly clear that these backroom Bhoys were a unit every bit as talented, well balanced and closely knit as the Lions themselves. 'Everyone had their strengths, their areas of expertise,' Sean would say. 'And above all, they were good men. Our personalities gelled well together. It was just a pleasure coming into work with them every day.'

"This chimed with what I later heard from the trio's families. 'They were as thick as thieves,' was how Neilly Jnr described them in an interview for Sean's book. 'That was my dad's happiest time at Celtic, when he was with Jock and Sean. They were just pals.'

Sean readily confirmed that assessment, adding that theirs was a small and exclusive circle. 'Jock was picky when it came to his friends. He didn't have many of them,' Fallon said. 'Trust was so important to him and he liked to be surrounded by folk he knew well. He was naturally suspicious of people and if he didn't like you - and there were plenty he didn't like - you knew all about it. What Jock really loved was to be among 'football men' as we called them, talking about the game, going into detail. You didn't get his respect or his trust easily but, once you had it, he would trust you with a lot.'

"The workloads of Fallon and Mochan reflected that. Yet Stein was not a delegator by nature. At Dunfermline and Hibernian, he had ploughed a lone furrow, at times actively shunning the input of others. 'Jock did it all on his own back then,' said Tommy Callaghan, who played under Stein at East End Park before joining him in Glasgow. 'It was much more of a team effort at Celtic, and you could see the trust he had in the likes of Sean and Neilly.' Trust. Respect. Even, whisper it, affection. When it came to Fallon and Mochan, his most senior and influential lieutenants, Stein had all three in abundance. And yet neither of these men were his appointments. Fallon, in fact, had been groomed for the manager's job before the alignment of Stein's successes and the Kelly Kids' failures forced Sir Robert's hand. Mochan, for his part - like Bob Rooney before him - had already been brought in at Fallon's urging. 'I knew Neilly would be a great trainer for the team and he certainly didn't let me down,' Sean told me. 'We became one of the fittest teams in Europe and he had a lot to do with that. I always felt we needed people like Neilly at Celtic.'

"Faced with a backroom team that had been hand-picked by others, Stein could have sidelined Fallon and Mochan, or at the very least restricted their influence. As it was, identifying their extraordinary talent in key areas, he took the opposite course and watched Celtic reap the benefits. Stein was always the undisputed leader; a magnificent manager of rare and, at the time, unparalleled abilities. But Celtic was no one-man show and, over time - albeit not by those closest to the success story - that become largely forgotten. As legend of Big Jock grew in the years following his premature death, so the colossal contributions of Fallon and Mochan became diminished. This airbrushing from history greatly irked many of the players who saw first-hand just how vital these men had been.

"Just think, for example, of Stein's Celtic without Mochan's nous at Barrowfield, and the energy and endurance that brought to the team. Then imagine that team without the Dalglishs and Gemmells, the Simpsons, McGrains, Connellys and many more besides, all of whom Fallon spotted, signed and helped nurture. Delve deeper still and contemplate Stein's abrasive management style without the complementary personalities of Smiler and the Iron Man, forever soothing disputes and healing divisions. If the prospect leaves you contemplating an era without such a golden hue, it should.

"I was amazed and genuinely awed that this failure to apportion credit, especially where it was so evidently due, never rankled with Sean. 'I wasn't in the job for recognition,' he would say. 'I was in the job to do my best for Celtic and to do what I thought would help make the club successful. I like to think I achieved that. No football club gets success without an awful lot of people doing their jobs right, and myself, Neilly and many others did our jobs well at that time. Jock was the boss and he was a tremendous leader for us all. But we all played our parts, and I'm sure Jock would have been the first to tell you that.'

"Sadly, Stein died before beginning work on a planned autobiography that would, one hopes, have conveyed his admiration and gratitude. The result is that Fallon and Mochan missed out on the kind of praise - lavish but fully merited - bestowed on the likes of Peter Taylor, Brian Clough's celebrated number two, and the members of Liverpool's fabled boot-room.

"Comparisons with the Anfield set-up have rarely been drawn, but seem particularly apt. After all, beyond the tight inner circle of Stein, Fallon, Mochan, Bob Rooney and Jimmy Steele, there existed at Celtic a wider network of friends, former team-mates and advisors. From John Higgins (chief scout) through coaches Willie Fernie and Alec Boden to John McAlindon (groundsman/maintenance), the club's backroom team was packed full of men who were known and, with the odd exception, implicitly trusted. All were former charges of Jimmy McGrory, who was himself a permanent fixture at Celtic Park along with another ex-player, supporters liaison officer Jim Kennedy. And most had formed part of Celtic's greatest team of the McGrory era: the 1953-54 double-winners.

"Stein had especially fond memories of that season, and Fallon recalled that his early plans were based of emulating the class of 54's spirit and togetherness. Like most of what Stein put his mind to, that goal was achieved in some style. It is beyond dispute that Celtic became, and remained, one of the greatest and most exhilarating teams of a golden football age.

"Yet if there is another incontestable aspect to those halcyon years, it is this. However dazzling the teams, however brilliant the manager, neither would have sparkled quite so brightly had it not been for the humble colossuses at Stein's side."

CHAPTER 11:

CELTIC AMORE

Gargantua was gone. Thirteen years under Jock Stein's guidance had bestowed Celtic with honours beyond its wildest dreams. That great servant, Sean Fallon, was also shown the door in less-than-dignified circumstances by a board which increasingly bred incredulity within the Celtic support. After a summer of discontent and irrevocable change, Neilly Mochan found himself as the sole survivor of the Lisbon magi. At 51 years of age, Smiler's role had evolved from trainer to include that of kit-man, sponge-man and ground-staff mentor but his familiar routine of boot-room pots of tea with his two great friends was now sadly a thing of the past. With Bobby Lennox having joined the lucrative NASL and landed in Houston, Neilly found himself as the last Lion in paradise.

Who could replace the irreplaceable? The press lauded the trio of Paddy Crerand, Bertie Auld and Billy McNeill. Each of these ex-Celts would have found a seamless fit within Neilly's boot-room for an after-match nip as the four men had lined up together for Jimmy McGrory's first-team as far back as 1958. Ultimately, it was announced that the great Cesar, at just 38 years of age – and only three years after retiring as a player - would take the helm.

The failure of Stein's final season identified the desperate need for reinforcements on the pitch. Mainstays of his 1977 double-winning side - Danny McGrain, Pat Stanton and Kenny Dalglish - had been lost and not replaced, and McNeill faced one of the greatest challenges of his career to prise the Premier League title back from Ibrox. The season that followed was to be one of the most dramatic in the history of Celtic Football Club.

Andy Lynch, who captained Celtic for much of the 1978-79 campaign, remembered fondly Mochan's influence on the club and its players. "Neilly was a gentleman in many ways and there are not many footballers from the modern day I could say that about. He was from a different era and I felt that, when I looked at Neilly, I was looking at Celtic and what it represented. He had been part of Jock Stein's backroom team and was very loyal to the club. He was a fairly quiet guy but you could see that he was enjoying what he was doing. As I read a bit of the club's history, I realised that he had been a fantastic player and had achieved some wonderful things in the game. But he was a very humble person.

"Neilly came from an age when men were mannerly and it was obvious to me that Celtic came first to him at all times. I would class him as one of the real workers at that football club and he was very proud to fulfil that role. He was 100% sincere and part of the team. He completely controlled the kit at Celtic Park. If you asked big Billy for something he would simply say, 'Ask Neilly, he's the boss.'

"He had scored that famous goal in the Coronation Cup final and whenever we played at Hampden, Neilly would start describing his strike. The boys would ask, 'How far out was it Neilly?' and he kept this going for years. He started off at around 30 yards but it got further back every year. Eventually he had hit it from the halfway line."

By the end of September 1978, McNeill's Celtic had won ten and lost just one of their League and League Cup matches. The new manager made moves in the transfer market and shrewdly re-signed the evergreen Bobby Lennox before breaking the domestic transfer record by paying £120,000 for Kilmarnock's 22-year-old winger Davie Provan. Some of that massive fee was recouped with the sales of Paul Wilson to Motherwell and Joe Craig to Blackburn Rovers as the boss began to craft his own Celtic side from the embers of Stein's last stand.

"Neilly had gone from being the trainer to the kit-man," remembered Bobby Lennox. "He was always in about the boot-room and you went to see him anytime you needed anything. He was a permanent fixture at the park and you could always go and speak to him. I don't ever remember Neilly having a day off. Every time you went into Celtic Park, he was there and if you walked into the changing room and some of the first team were about, Neilly would say, 'Here's one of the good players coming.' He could embarrass you that way."

"Billy and John Clark were the management team and Neilly was the old-fashioned trainer when I joined," recalled Davie Provan. "If there was an injury on the pitch, he was the guy who ran on and he took great pride in the pace that he could get to you. He used to sprint on with the magic sponge in his bag and was always very dismissive of you if you had an injury. It was more or less, 'Get back on your feet, there's nothing wrong with you.' You could be lying there with a compound fracture and Neilly would be telling you to get back up. Every injury was treated with the wet sponge because that's all he had. Brian Scott eventually succeeded Bob Rooney as the physiotherapist as Billy brought him down from Aberdeen. No disrespect to Bob but he was more old-school and Scotty was very much into sports science and was very progressive.

"I remember walking into training for the first couple of days at Celtic Park and Neilly was there. I wished him good morning and he answered, 'Morning James'. I went in the following day and said, 'Hi Neilly,' to which he again responded, 'Morning James'. So for about the first two months he called me James and this was Neilly Mochan telling me that he didn't even know who I was, just in case there was any chance of me getting big-headed about the record transfer fee. That was one of Neilly's great gifts, he never allowed anyone to get ahead of themselves. He was the master at bringing people down.

"We used to get changed at Celtic Park and take the cars or run up to Barrowfield. It was a Rangers fan who owned the yard behind the goals and he would burn tyres so the smoke would blow across the training ground. People would often say that it was good enough for the Lisbon Lions but they won the European Cup despite Barrowfield, not because of it. The first time I saw the place, I couldn't believe that it was Celtic's training facility because even Kilmarnock had two or three really good training pitches behind their stadium. Celtic had won the European Cup 11 years previously and they were training on a mud heap.

"Neilly was still fit enough to do the warm up with us. He would jog around with us and give us a good stretch to get us prepared to train and then Billy, John and Frank Connor would come in and do the sessions. I was surprised when I first went into the dressing room and it was half the size of the one at Kilmarnock. They still had the old circular-headed showers with the stone floor. The facilities were basic to say the least and the changing room was freezing cold. We used to have ice on the inside of the dressing room windows but it didn't do us any harm.

"The day I made my debut at Firhill, I got off the bus and went to walk into the front door of the stadium and Neilly shouted me back. I turned around and he said, 'Hampers.' He took me around the back of the bus and made me carry the kit hampers into Firhill and that was Neilly. I thought at first that he was going to make my life a misery but when you got to know him you realised that he was terrific at keeping everyone's feet on the ground. Once you earned his respect he was completely different with you and all the new players got the same initiation.

"Billy spoke to me after I made my debut. My first involvement in the game came when somebody switched the ball out to me on the right and I brought my body up, took the ball down and quickly whipped in a cross that came away from the 'keeper. Billy told me that when I did that, Neilly had said to him, 'It's years since I've seen someone doing that,' and he was laughing when he said it because he used to do that when he got excited. Billy mentioned that to me after the game and I took that as a great compliment from Neilly Mochan."

The acquisition of the combative Murdo MacLeod, a promising 20-year-old midfielder signed from Dumbarton for £100,000 in November 1978, added further competition to Billy McNeill's midfield. However, as Celtic prepared for their League Cup semi-final against Rangers on 13th December 1978, their league form had taken something of a dip and a domestic cup looked to be the club's best chance of silverware in this season of transition.

All who ever worked with Neilly Mochan would testify that he was a consummate professional and his preparations for matches were meticulous in the extreme. He was also heavily involved in the pre-match routine of relaxing players with massages and walks as well as preparing the squad's kit. Regardless of such commitments, the Camelon native always found time to assist local Celtic fans and supporter's clubs with big-match tickets as brother Denis recalled, "The amount of tickets he managed to get for people was unbelievable. On the Friday night before a big game there used to be priests and everything down at the house looking for tickets." James Butler remembered supporter's buses from Fife stopping on their way through to Glasgow on the off-chance that Neilly could help them out, "The buses would stop on the corner and they would jump over the fence and knock on the kitchen window. My auntie Mary would pass the tickets to them out the window. Stephen Gallacher [professional golfer and 2014 Ryder Cup winner] used to go to the games with his uncle and they always got their tickets off Neilly. Jim Kennedy was head of the ticket office and even he used to go to Neilly for tickets on a Saturday."

Celtic were built on tradition and Billy McNeill stuck to many of the routines favoured by his predecessor as he took his squad to Seamill to prepare for the third Old Firm encounter of his managerial reign. "Seamill was great," recalled Davie Provan. "That was the one place where you could get away from it all and get your head around the game. Nobody was bothering you and asking for tickets and the married boys got away from the screaming kids and could get a bit of concentration. We would go down for a few days and Neilly would phone Bunnie Wilkie, the Largs bookie, to come down to the hotel and take the boys' bets. It was great fun and pretty productive in terms of the trophies that we won. Seamill was kind to Celtic. It was a bit dilapidated but big Jock loved it and that's why they started going down there. Billy maintained that tradition and the boys loved the place, even though it was a bit like *Fawlty Towers*. I remember rooming with Mike Conroy before the League Cup semi-final and I never got one wink of sleep because of his snoring. You wouldn't dare ask for your own room because Neilly would have been on your case.

"Before the morning of a big game, the tradition was that Neilly took us a walk from Seamill down to Portencross. It was a couple of miles there and back and I think that big Jock had Neilly doing that for years, just to blow the cobwebs away and get your head around the game before you went on the team bus.

"Everybody had their function and Jimmy Steele was the one who would crack the jokes and play the fool before the big games and that would ease the tension. He played the court jester and people used to think that he was daft but he was far from it. I could see why Jock Stein loved to have him around because before the really important games you need somebody to do what Steelie did. He would crack a joke with somebody or grab a waitress and start dancing with her at the pre-match meal just to get the boys laughing, and he was terrific at it."

Celtic failed to reach their 15th consecutive League Cup final as Rangers won an enthralling match 3-2 after extra time, and by the end of the year McNeill's new-look side were languishing in sixth place of a ten-team league. A three-month spell of frozen pitches meant that no further league matches would be played until March 1979 and this left Celtic with a hectic fixture pile-up in the run-in to one of the biggest showdowns in the history of the Old Firm derby. A run of 17 league games in 10 weeks resulted in 13 wins, one draw and three defeats and clawed the Bhoys back into contention for the title. McNeill's side entered their final league game of the season at home against Rangers requiring a win to claim the championship crown. John Greig's visitors, for their part, needed a draw to keep their title aspirations alive. The 90 minutes that ensued is now simply referred to in the scrolls of Celtic history as 'the 4-2 game,' when ten men won the league.

"There were five of us on the ground-staff," recalled Charlie Nicholas. "As well as myself, there was Danny Crainie, Willie McStay, Gerry Crawley and a boy from Castlemilk called Hugh Ferry. On the day of the 4-2 game we had a plan to get some Celtic jerseys from Neilly Mochan so that we could wear them to the game that night. You never got one over on him and I think he knew that we were up to something that day because he was always one step ahead of you. He kept absolutely everything in his stashes and so we were hanging about the park waiting for him to leave and he just gave us that look and told us to enjoy the game that night. With the coast clear, we went into the dressing room and there were five extra jerseys laid out. I'm sure he did it on purpose because he knew us better than we knew ourselves. So we grabbed the jerseys and put them in a bag. That night we were all in the Jungle at Celtic Park wearing authentic Celtic tops to watch our team winning the league. The fans had no idea who we were, why would they? But they kept commenting on the hoops' tops we had on. It made an already special night even better for us and that was down to The Moch. Of course, we were in the following day and we had to smuggle the tops back in to Neilly's stash. He just asked us if we had enjoyed the game but he had that look in his eye and he knew what we had been up to."

"Billy McNeill did really well to take over from Jock," asserted Davie Provan. "You needed someone of real stature to take on that job and Billy was the one who had the presence to do it. We had a good mix in that team. Danny McGrain was the top man and he had an ankle injury when I signed and that kept him out for over a year. But he was still there throughout the season and was revered by everyone at the club. Andy Lynch was a good, hardworking pro and we had further experience in Peter Latchford and Bobby Lennox, who came back at the age of 36 and was still at the front in training. Billy kept the players he trusted and hunted the ones he didn't want. I think he felt that he needed fresh legs and there was a great mixture of the experienced players and the likes of myself, George McCluskey, Tommy Burns, Roy Aitken, Mike Conroy and Murdo MacLeod. The younger boys gave that team the legs and the older ones gave us the wisdom.

"It was the best part of my professional life being in that dressing room. I've played in better Celtic teams but I've never been in a better dressing room than that first season. I've got a great picture of the whole group in the changing room after the 4-2 game. In the corner of the room is Neilly Mochan and he is just beaming with pride. He was never usually overly emotional but I think the 4-2 game even got to Neilly. He was a bit emotional that night, as we all were, but he was made up for us. He had such a great love for the club."

Celtic relinquished their league title the following season by a single point to Alex Ferguson's Aberdeen. It was the first time the championship trophy had left Glasgow since 1965 and was a sure sign that a New Firm revolution was underway in Scottish football. McNeill broke the transfer record in March 1980 to secure the signature of Liverpool's Frank McGarvey for £250,000 and Provan remembered how Mochan continued to keep everyone grounded. "Frank scored a hat-trick in one game and was talking about his goals after the game. Typically, Neilly said to him, 'You wouldn't even get to carry the hampers for the good team.' 'The good team' was the Lisbon Lions. Neilly never called them the Lions. If anyone was getting remotely carried away or too big for their boots, Neilly was the man to sort them out."

A successful European Cup run resulted in Celtic reaching the quarter-final stage, where Real Madrid overturned a 2-0 first-leg deficit to win the tie 3-2 in the Bernabeu. But that defeat left a sour taste in the mouth of Davie Provan. "The most disappointing thing about the second-leg against Real Madrid was the performance of the referee. Santillana went right through big Peter Latchford for their first goal and it should have been a free kick but the goal was given. It was right on the stroke of half time and it changed the whole complexion of the tie because they hadn't created a single chance in that first half."

McNeill's brave side were forced to lick their wounds, and a Scottish Cup win against Rangers, marred by crowd violence, provided some consolation at the end of a somewhat disappointing season. The scorer of Celtic's winning Hampden goal came from a proud and illustrious line of home-grown talents and the 22-year-old George McCluskey finished McNeill's second season as the club's top goalscorer. Season 1980-81 would see big Billy getting the better of Alex Ferguson in the title stakes once again. He would also unleash another prodigy in Charlie Nicholas, who won the Celtic faithful's hearts and was regarded by McNeill as the most naturally talented youngster he had ever worked with.

"We got Charlie, Paul McStay, Danny Crainie, Mark Reid and big Packie Bonner all breaking through at roughly the same time," pointed out Davie Provan. "Celtic took it for granted that we got three or four boys out of the youth teams coming through every year. Charlie adored Neilly because he had been one of his ground-staff boys and all those young boys looked up to Neilly. He was a pretty hard taskmaster with them but they loved him. Now and again when Charlie was in the first team he would start singing, 'When the ball hits the net at the speed of a jet, that's the Mochan' and the whole team would join in. Neilly would turn bright red because he was such a modest man and he got embarrassed. I think he was quite chuffed at the same time and the boys would sing this at the top of their voices and he'd be sitting there beaming away. The remarkable thing about Neilly was that he was loathe to talk about his own career. The two words that come to mind with him are modesty and humility. He would kid us on about the Coronation Cup final goal but very rarely would he open up about his career."

CHAPTER 12:

A GROUNDING IN PARADISE

Charlie Nicholas was the latest in a long line of Neilly's ground-staff boys to make his mark in the first-team, following on from previous alumni such as George Connelly, Brian McLaughlin and Tommy Burns. "I went into Celtic Park as a young boy and I cannot overstate the importance of Neilly on my development as a football player and as a human being," enthused Nicholas. "We called him 'The Moch' and he taught us what it meant to be part of this wonderful football club. We thought the world of Neilly and we would have done anything for him. He was hard on us, don't get me wrong. He really made us work on the ground-staff and he taught us the standards that he expected from us every single day at the park. He was a figure that I was already aware of because I was a Celtic fan growing up but what he did for that club long after his playing and training days were over was unbelievable, and a lot of people outside of Celtic Park didn't realise that because of the way he was. He never courted attention for all his efforts and achievements. It was The Moch who instilled the values of the club in us from a young age and he did that by setting an example to us. What a class act that man was. Everything went through Neilly at Celtic Park then. I know it sounds unusual now but people would go to him for something before they went to the manager. He was the heartbeat of that football club. Every player absolutely adored him, and he loved Celtic. Senior players revered him and they had to go to him cap-in-hand and ask for new football boots. The only player who had a boot deal was Danny McGrain but we used to watch how he was with the experienced players and realised early on that his word around the park was gospel. By the time we were playing we knew that the number one priority was to win. He gave us that winning mentality from a young age and we carried it on through the levels until we made it to the first team. The Moch really looked after his ground-staff boys and he made every day special to me. Even now they are the most cherished memories I have from my football career. All I ever wanted to do was pull on those green-and-white hoops and Neilly inspired me on so many levels to achieve that ambition. When people ask me about Celtic legends, I put Neilly Mochan at the very top every time."

As Nicholas was making his debut under Billy McNeill, another young hopeful was being taught the Celtic ways by Neilly Mochan. "I joined the club as a 15-year-old," remembered Peter Grant. "I was just out of school and still wet behind the ears. Neilly was the boss of the ground-staff and he was a legend to me. I knew what he had done as a player and as part of the 1967 team, so to join the ground-staff and be looked after by him was something special. He made every day a fun day but he was also very disciplined in what was expected from us, and his knowledge of football was incredible. There were only four or five of us on the ground-staff at that time including Owen Archdeacon and John Sludden. Neil was already there when we arrived in the morning and he always had jobs for us. Every day before we left, the dressing room had to be mopped, cleaned and hosed and the training gear had to be washed and put in the drier. He would say, 'Son' - that was his favourite word - 'Son, if the gear's not inside out or not folded the right way, then just leave it on the floor where they've put it.' You were in a position where you did what Neilly told you and this was senior players' kit we were talking about. I learned so much from Neil. He taught me all about respect and to knock on the first-team dressing room door to make sure it was ok before I walked in. I can honestly say that it was the best time of my life.

"I would be in there for about eight in the morning and I wouldn't leave until about five or six at night and Neilly would go around and check that everything was done. If a player hadn't untied the laces of their boots then that's the way they would pick them up the next day. All the disciplines were there in him. But he was also a funny man with such a dry sense of humour. He'd take Vaseline out the jar and put some on his hair and sweep it right back and then he would rub some on your elbows if we weren't brushing or mopping the floor well enough and tell us it was elbow grease. He would get one of the boys to hold the fire extinguisher with the nozzle pointing to the floor and tell him that we had to dry the floor with it. He told them to hold on to it until he plugged it in and the boy would be standing there holding the nozzle down waiting on it coming on. Then he would send one of the young boys to the chip shop on the corner of London Road and tell him to pick up a tonne of chips. One of the boys actually managed it one day and came up the road carrying twenty bags of chips and told Neilly he was away to pick up another five bags. He was hilarious day after day.

"He used to pick Derek Whyte up in Cumbernauld and the back windows of his car would be rolled down. Neil said they weren't working properly and would tell him to sit in the back seat. The rain would be lashing in from the open windows hitting Derek all the way to Glasgow and Neil would sit in the front with the hood of his snorkel up and not even look back but Whytey wouldn't dare to try and put the windows up.

"Boys would come in and ask for Adidas World Cup boots and Neil would say, 'Listen son, you won't be here long enough to get a pair of World Cups. You put these Adidas 2000 on with the big studs. That's the type of player you are.' First-team players would come in and ask for a new pair of boots and Neil would go up his ladders to one of his stashes and get them a new pair. They'd try them on and very rarely would tell him they were a bit tight and you could tell that they didn't want to tell him. So he'd go back into his cupboard and he'd change the box but give the player the same boots and ask them to try them on again for size. 'Aye Neil, they're a bit better,' and they'd be away with the same boots. Neilly never gave anything away, he had strips from the '50s in that cupboard still in their cellophane.

"I think Neil respected Celtic so much and he was very much part of their best ever team and when you look at the ground-staff boys he looked after, we all had one thing in common: we loved Celtic and the club was our life. We only ever wanted to play in one place and that is what Neil instilled in us all. I wasn't the greatest player by a long shot but he treated me the same way that he treated all of those players that went before me. He knew that every day I would have fought like a lion to pull on that Celtic jersey and that I worked hard every day to try and achieve that. Neil would not have accepted someone taking shortcuts and if he saw that attitude in one of his ground-staff boys then the manager would know all about it. We all wanted to be there and it was people like Neil Mochan that we wanted to follow.

"If he told me to jump I would have asked, 'How high?' If he saw that you had the desire and commitment to his club then he would have given you a big chance. I have no doubt that the manager would have asked Neil about certain players. Neil was probably the biggest psychologist you could get because he could figure out if you had the mentality to play for Celtic Football Club. I know that if I had stepped out of line once then Neilly would have told the manager not to touch me because he wanted players to represent this great club the way it should be represented. He gave his ground-staff boys the desire to play for one club and one club only."

John Sludden was also on the ground-staff in the early eighties and knew Neilly Mochan better than most. "First and foremost he was my uncle Neilly before I went to Celtic Park, and when I went in as a player he was 'The Moch'," explained Sludden. "He just completely changed, as if he was in his comfort zone. He was shy away from the park but when he went there his personality was unbelievable. He was the life and soul of the place and I think he was very relaxed there. He was probably the biggest wind-up merchant I've ever met in my life but he had a soft spot for all of the ground-staff boys. He looked after them and helped them along the way in their careers. When you look at the history of the club, Neilly was involved in all the great occasions be it as player, coach or kit-man. He was a Celtic legend but he always spoke to the players about the importance of the supporters. He gave his time to the supporters' clubs whenever he could.

"I was playing in a Youth Cup final and I had to go and ask Neilly for a pair of boots. He said to me, 'Listen son, if you look in that trophy room, there's a cup in there with big ears. We went to Lisbon and won that cup without new boots and you want a pair for a Youth Cup final?' I just had to walk away after that.

"Neilly would drop off Paul and Willie McStay at the bus stop beside the old Glasgow Zoo after training. They were both in the first team at this point and I remember he used to drive right passed the stop and on to the motorway before saying to them, 'Where are you going tonight boys? Are you coming to Falkirk with us?' One of the McStays would say that they had missed their stop and Neilly would pull up on the side of the motorway and ask, 'What did you not say for, son?' and drop them off. Here was Paul McStay, the best prospect in British football, and Neilly made him walk along the motorway for half-a-mile to his bus stop."

Paul McStay made the first-team breakthrough as Celtic won their second successive championship in 1981-82. It was McNeill's third in four seasons as manager, and Aberdeen were again the runners-up. Behind the glory, tragedy befell the Celtic family on 19th October 1981 as Johnny Doyle died in a tragic accident in his home at the age of only 30. He was a player who was much loved by Mochan, as Pat Stanton explained. "Johnny was full of fun and you never knew what was coming next from him as he was always pulling pranks. Neilly loved Doyley because he was a wee bit like him. They liked a laugh and they liked to kid people on but they knew where to draw the line. You get all that during the week but come a Saturday in the dressing room, these guys were switched on to something else. They had great determination and you need these people in the changing room."

Charlie Nicholas recovered from a broken leg sustained the previous season to become the most sought-after young player in British football. Each of his incredible 46 goals for Celtic during a vintage 1982-83 campaign added further weight to his value, and the board were predictably keen to sell. The 22-year-old was named Scotland's Player of the Year and helped the club to a League Cup win over Rangers, although the league was again lost by a single point, this time to Dundee United. Nicholas left for Arsenal for £750,000 and, despite winning three league titles in five seasons, Billy McNeill followed him on that familiar path from Parkhead to England, becoming manager of Manchester City. For the second time in five years, Celtic were on the look-out for a new manager. With McNeill and Clark gone, Neilly and reserve-team coach Bobby Lennox also provided the final links to Lisbon.

"When I took over as manager, you could still source good Scottish players from within the club," stated Davie Hay, who became Celtic's sixth manager in July 1983. "Exceptional players like Charlie Nicholas, Roy Aitken and Paul McStay had recently come through the system before I arrived and we had a decent team. Neilly was actually quite quiet when I was a player there and I got to know him better when I came back as manager. I asked him if he wanted to help us with training again but he was happy being the kit-man at that stage of his career. I would still have quiet talks with him and he would give his opinion when asked but he would never offer it, such was his way. One thing that he always instilled in players was the importance of beating Rangers and that was clearly a big factor with Neilly. I liked him a lot and people of his ilk are vitally important to the history and traditions of Celtic. I don't think that should ever be lost."

In Davie Hay's debut term in charge, and for the first time since 1978, Celtic endured a trophyless campaign. With his darling striker Charlie

Nicholas en route to Highbury, McNeill had acted quickly to draft in 19-year-old Motherwell striker Brian McClair for under a tenth of the fee received from Arsenal. This was a player Hay would be glad to have inherited, as the new Bhoy scored an impressive 31 goals in his maiden season. "Neilly made a huge impact on me from the very beginning," recalled McClair. "I remember vividly my first experience of him. He asked me on the first or second day which kind of boots I would like. I asked him for Adidas World Cups and he just looked at me and started laughing at me in a Mochan way in front of everybody. He started pointing at me and saying, 'What do you think of this, eh? Just in the door and he wants World Cups?' I was totally mortified but he just left it at that and I went out and trained. After training he came in and gave me the boots and it's only when I look back that I realise what he was doing and he was absolutely right. I had obviously come in as a smart arse and he was putting me exactly where I should have been put. From that moment on it made a big difference to my attitude and I realised that I knew nothing and had better be careful.

"All the senior pros loved him because they had been young players under Neilly's tutelage in the past and they had been party to, and sometimes victims of, many of his practical jokes. He had a real sharp sense of humour and I never saw Neilly without a smile on his face for the four years that I was there. He was so positive and a terrific person to have around. Part of his own entertainment was that during a game he would throw a few things in the manager's ear to see if he would get a nibble. More often than not he would and the gaffer would jump out and shout at the players or the linesman or the referee. Meanwhile Neilly would be killing himself laughing at the back of the dugout, looking at the other guys and winking at them because he had done it again.

"It was important to have someone like Neilly at the football club who knew what the values were. He taught me that I had to earn the right at a club like Celtic, and that thread also ran through Manchester United. It went right back to the Second World War and through the national service that guys like that went through. That would have been part of the reason that Neilly was so immaculate. He had the kit-man's coat, his hair was done, he was clean-shaven, he smelt fantastic. He always looked the part and everything he did was done to the best of his ability."

Another ground-staff boy who shared a real affinity with Mochan was Stuart Balmer. "Neilly gave us every task you could imagine around the stadium," remembered Stuart. "If the game was going to be televised, he would come out with the Tippex and tell us to get all the Adidas stripes and all the Nike ticks painted white because some of the players had sponsors. He was quite secretive with what he kept in his little cubbie holes and he didn't give much away. He would tell you that if you wanted to keep warm then you had to run about. God knows what he had in that Alladin's cave of his.

"He was a really jovial guy who loved a laugh and you would never have realised what he achieved at the club unless you looked through the history books because he was just an ordinary guy who liked a wee bet on his horses. It was great being around him and he was always taking the mickey out of someone, be it the young boys, the first-team or even the management. He kept everyone on their toes.

"Neilly would run the old bath for us and get in first. Little did we know that he had turned on the scalding hot tap. He would be sitting in the bath washing his hair because he could somehow handle the heat. As soon as we touched the water we'd be straight back out and he'd let out that laugh of his. He'd get out and get dried and then put football socks on with the ties, then his Doc Marten's shoes and then his tracksuit bottoms. Then he'd put the Vaseline in his hair and comb his hair. That was his hair gel. He went through that same routine every day.

"I remember on the night of a Wednesday European game, Neilly told me that he needed to get the ball dried for the Saturday. He told me to put it in the tumble drier and so I went and did it. He was standing scratching his back off the corner of the wall as he always did and he was laughing his head off at me with his 'hee, hee, hee, hee' laugh.

"Alex Mathie and I were allowed to travel in with Neilly once we earned the right. I came from Bainsford so it wasn't too far from him but we had to prove our loyalty and reliability to him first. That was another part of the grounding that we got from him and I think it stood us in good stead over the years."

"He kept everyone on their toes," remembered Davie Provan. "If you went to Neilly for a pair of boots, you had to have holes in your old ones before you'd get a pair. I remember my toes were sticking out both feet and this was in April. I was still using the pair of boots I had started with at the beginning of the season and I asked for a new pair of boots. He just looked at my boots and said, 'This is April son. I can't give you a new pair of boots because I hear they're going to free you at the end of the season.' I was looking at him and he was brilliant at keeping a straight face and then of course he started creasing himself laughing. That was Neilly, he was a wind-up merchant and brilliant at keeping a straight face."

Davie was given his new boots and used his right one to devastating effect to breathe new life into Davie Hay's managerial career the following month. The 1984-85 league title had already been lost to Aberdeen when Celtic lined up to face Dundee United in the 100th Scottish Cup final. With Hay's team trailing to a Stuart Beedie goal with just 14 minutes remaining, Provan wrapped his Nike boot around a direct free-kick and curled the ball into Hamish McAlpine's top-left hand corner. Frank McGarvey's header settled the tie eight minutes later and Hay sampled his first success in the Celtic dugout. As enjoyable an occasion as it was, it was clear that the Glasgow giants could not go three years without a league crown and so the following campaign would prove pivotal for the Quality Street Kid-turned-gaffer.

Before Hay was able to taste championship success, Celtic and the world of football were to lose one of its all-time greatest figures. "Jock had gone into the park before travelling down to Cardiff with the Scottish national team," remembered James Butler. "He would do that fairly often because, first and foremost, Neilly and Jock were friends. They kept in touch when they both left Celtic the first time around and that continued after Jock left as manager. Stein valued Neilly's opinion on football matters and he would go into his boot-room to sit for hours drinking tea. But on this particular occasion, Neilly was dreadfully worried about him. He said he didn't look well at all and that he was ashen-faced. He was so concerned that he asked Doctor Fitzsimons to check him over, and Jock was told not to travel down to Wales."

Stein did not, of course, heed the doctor's orders and suffered a fatal heart attack as his Scotland side secured a World Cup finals play-off spot on 10th September 1985. Scottish football would be forever in his shadow. "Neilly always said that Celtic Park was never the same after Jock left," continued James Butler. "But he lost his great friend that night and that friendship went beyond football."

The response from Hay's Celtic was typically dramatic as they fought out a fierce championship battle with Hearts, a team that hadn't won the league since Stein was the manager of Dunfermline in 1960. The title race went down to the wire and, on the final day of the season, Hearts travelled to Dens Park with a two-point cushion. A draw would have given them the title and their goal difference was also four superior to Celtic's. Of the Hoops side praying for a miracle against St Mirren at Love Street, all but Murdo MacLeod, Brian McClair and Mo Johnston had graduated from the Celtic Park stable.

"I shouldn't have been in the Love Street dugout that day," admitted Davie Provan. "I was in civvies and wasn't even on the bench. I had been in the stand but the minute Albert Kidd scored the first goal for Dundee against Hearts, I made my way down to the dugout to sit with Neilly and Steelie. I hadn't felt part of it because I had been out for quite a long time leading up to that game so I went down to feel more part of what was happening. To be fair to Davie Hay, he could have chased me but he let me sit there and the boys kept looking over and asking what the score was. Even if Hearts lost 1-0, we needed to win 3-0 just to be level with them and then Albert Kidd scored his second for Dundee and I put my two fingers up to let the guys know on the pitch. It was an amazing day and Neilly would have been the calmest man in that dugout."

McClair scored Celtic's fifth in a spectacular 5-0 win to secure the league championship in a fashion that only Celtic could. "Neilly loved being part of it," the former striker recalled. "He would be sitting in the changing room after that game with a smile. He was there during some amazing experiences in Celtic's history. He gave me a challenge when I was a young player and made me realise what I had to aspire to. When you think of what he achieved as a player, trainer and then kit-man, Neilly Mochan is a legend."

CHAPTER 13:

CELTIC CENTURION

As the extended Mochan family settled down in Neil and Mary's Camelon home to celebrate the former's 60th birthday in April 1987, the fortunes of Celtic were never far from their minds. The weekend's 3-1 victory over Rangers was the topical subject of conversation as Andy Cameron appeared on the television screen in the corner of the living room to lament his team's failure to end Celtic's 1986-87 championship hopes. Frank Carson, who had also attended the match in the green-and-white end of the stadium, was indulging Cameron with a discussion on events when he announced to the Scottish TV audience, "Without Neilly Mochan, there is no Celtic." Buoyant cheers erupted in the living room and Neilly, who had been up the loft fetching some alcohol for his guests a short time before, turned to nephew, James Butler, and whispered in his ear, "James, you'll need to take a look at the bedroom ceiling during the week; I've put my foot right through it." Always happiest when surrounded by family and never one to court attention, this was vintage Neilly.

Rangers' Graeme Souness-inspired side eventually did win the league with six points to spare that season, and Davie Hay paid dearly for a trophyless campaign with the loss of his job. The return of Cesar coincided with Celtic's upcoming centenary celebrations but Billy McNeill undertook a huge rebuilding job as he lost a host of vital figures: Danny McGrain had been freed after 20 years service and signed for Hamilton Academical; Davie

Provan retired after a lengthy battle with ME; top goalscorer Brian McClair joined Alex Ferguson's Manchester United revolution; Mo Johnston moved to France and FC Nantes; Murdo MacLeod also left for foreign shores with a transfer to Borussia Dortmund; and Alan McInally's departure took him to Aston Villa. With half a team on the way out, McNeill had to work quickly, and the shrewd acquisition of the versatile and experienced Billy Stark from Aberdeen in July 1987 proved a masterstroke.

"I was very fortunate that circumstances worked for me when big Billy was installed as manager and needed to bring in some players," the goalscoring midfielder recalled. "Big Billy knew of me, having been a competitor against Celtic with Saint Mirren and Aberdeen and, luckily for me, he felt that I could come in and do a job. I came in from an Aberdeen team which had been successful and that was a good position to be in when joining a club like Celtic, who are expected to win every game and to have trophies in the cabinet at the end of the season.

"When I came to the club, Billy McNeill had Tommy Craig as his assistant and Neilly Mochan was the kit-man. Being a reasonable student of Scottish football, I knew all about Neilly and that he had a huge amount of experience and success as a player. I knew he had played for Scotland in the World Cup Finals and, although he played through some lean years for Celtic, he was certainly a factor in the 7-1 League Cup and Coronation Cup successes. Then he became part of the backroom staff. Having regularly played against Celtic, you always bumped into him when he was busy doing his work around the dressing room, so I knew of him but I didn't know him personally. It was probably indicative of Neilly that there wasn't one particular moment that I remember meeting him because he was very unassuming and he just went about his work, but he was a real character. I think he played a huge part in Celtic's history, both as a player and also as part of the backroom staff during the Jock Stein years. To try and sum him up when I was there, I would say the words that come to mind are wise, knowledgeable and unassuming. For me, Neilly was very underestimated in terms of the part that he played in Celtic's achievements over the years after his playing career ended. Neilly was a calming influence, that is the type of character that he was.

"When I look back at the job that Billy McNeill had in front of him, where Graeme Souness had come in and revolutionised Scottish football in terms of the money that he was able to spend, Celtic were expected to live with that and to at least match it. But we didn't have the funds that Rangers had. That's all been part of recent history and Celtic maybe had the biscuit tin philosophy which became a standing joke. But I'm sure that Billy would tell you that it was a huge bonus for him to have Neilly Mochan there. That consistency that was always there and someone who had done it all.

"Although he was a quiet, unassuming guy, nobody stepped over the line with Neilly because he could cut you down with a one-liner. I think that's the other thing that I remember about him during the years that I was there. New players came in and everybody's a different type of character and you would get quieter ones, and I would probably put myself in that category, but there were also the ebullient ones and the players full of personality that you absolutely need, like McAvennie. But if they were getting a wee bit above themselves then Neilly took it upon himself to bring them down to earth a wee bit and sometimes it only took one line. I can't recall Neilly ever raising his voice, I really can't, and I think that's the measure of him. The authority that he had without having to do that was absolutely there and everybody recognised it and respected it.

"If I was to look back over my career, that season for me was the highlight. We knew what was in front of us in terms of expectations and I don't think anybody had us as favourites because Graeme Souness was bringing in English international players to fill the squad at Ibrox, so we knew that it was going to be tough. I think the thing that was very important to us that season was the spirit and big Billy installed that in us. The players who had come up from England very quickly learned what Celtic was all about. Socially that season, there was not a weekend that we weren't out at Celtic supporter's events, and Billy insisted on that. He was of the belief that they were the most important people and the players were expected to go and show them that they were part of the club. Neilly was part of that backroom staff who gelled everybody very quickly. Neilly did it in his own quiet way and I think the important thing to point out was, although he wasn't loud, he had a terrific sense of humour and loved a laugh. With the celebrations, he was part of the team and you could see that he loved Celtic and he loved Celtic being successful, but I never saw him showing that in a way that was over-the-top. I think that was something that added to his authority. When you see someone like Neilly, who had been there and seen and done it all, and you're maybe getting carried away in the moment, he never behaved like it was really a big deal. I think he quite liked putting that across because he never spoke about his career but you sort of knew that he had that up his sleeve if he needed it.

"Neilly had a fantastic sense of humour and he used to travel through from the Falkirk area with some of the young boys, who were in awe of him because he was a local hero as well. In the middle of winter he would roll down the back window where they were sitting and he would force them to sit there freezing all the way through to Celtic Park. They never said a word and just put up with it and Neilly would be chortling away to himself in the front seat. It was unfortunate that I only came to know Neilly from going as a player at an older age, but everybody had total respect for the man."

Billy McNeill had captured a young Brian McClair from Motherwell in 1983 but the manager had left Celtic Park before getting the opportunity to work with the prolific marksman, who went onto become the club's top goalscorer for four seasons in succession before making Celtic a profit of £775,000. The Fir Park outfit were again plundered by McNeill in 1987 as he sought a replacement to fill the void left by McClair and his striking partner Maurice Johnston, who between them had scored no fewer than 70 goals in the previous fruitless season. Andy Walker was the young Celtic-supporting striker bequeathed with the unenviable task of filling the No.9 shorts, and he remembered his arrival fondly.

"I've got fabulous memories of coming to Celtic," said Walker. "It was July '87 and I had pretty much been tapped up because my old man had been in contact with one of the directors, Jim Farrell, and I was at Motherwell at the time. He had approached my old man around the February and asked if I would be interested in going to Celtic, and my dad didn't tell me until we were knocked out of the Scottish Cup. We had a pretty decent year that season at Motherwell and we got knocked out in the quarter-finals by

Dundee United and then my old man told me that Celtic were going to come and get me in the summer and I played the last few months at Motherwell with a huge smile on my face because the prospect of signing for Celtic was just fabulous. I've got to say I was a bit star-struck going into a dressing room full of my heroes because Celtic were my team. I'm one of 11 children, there's seven boys in our house, and my old man had taken us to games since I was five or six years old. Some of our best memories as a family are jumping over the gate and going to watch Celtic in big games against Rangers, big games in Europe, semi-finals and cup finals at Hampden. My childhood memories are full of all that and in fact big Billy's last game, the '75 cup final against Airdrie, was one of the first big games I was at. My whole childhood was dominated by fabulous Celtic memories, so to go into a dressing room where not only was big Billy the manager, but I was pretty much playing alongside some of my heroes, was absolutely fantastic. Paul McStay, who was the same age as me but I had been watching him play for Celtic for years, Roy Aitken, Pat Bonner, Tommy Burns. Some fabulous names that had been at Celtic for so long and had played in successful teams. And that was all that I was interested in - I just wanted to be part of the team and part of a team that had success. Billy took me aside when he signed me for between £350,000 and £400,000 and he said, 'I'm not going to make a big splash about you signing. Davie Provan is retiring so we're going to announce that and I'm also going to announce the signing of Billy Stark and that should take the pressure off you. Then I'll bring you in'. I remember it as if it was yesterday because it was fabulous and I was getting married that year, so my wife was really happy because I signed for Celtic. We got married shortly after that and we had two days up at Gleneagles for our honeymoon and then I went for ten days to Sweden with Celtic.

"Those were great days, really great days and you were just wondering what was awaiting you, how are you going to fit in? Were you going to fit in? And how was the team going to do because Rangers were spending a lot of money and they had a right good side. Big Billy had come back and there were so many changes but I was in the same boat as Billy Stark, Chris Morris and Mick McCarthy, who were all new players but we were made to feel really welcome. It was a great setup with a great bunch of boys and training was terrific. I really enjoyed pre-season."

Having finally made the transition from Celtic fan to player, Walker was welcomed to the club by a figure he had revered for most of his life. Neilly Mochan witnessed this young man entering Celtic Park full of dreams and expectations and had welcomed so many like him into the fold for over 20 years as the gatekeeper of Paradise. Neilly was about to make or break another new recruit "Everyone who was a Celtic fan knew Neilly and his history and the goals that he scored and that fabulous left foot of his, and when I first came up to the ground, I pretty much came up with nothing," Walker recalled. "I went in very early because I didn't want to be late in anyway, so I went down to the ground for about quarter-to-nine when we were to be in for about ten o' clock. There was no-one else in and Neilly came into the dressing room and asked me how I was and we had a bit of chat. He told me that we were going up to Strathclyde Park for training. I was braced for all that but all I had were training shoes and I asked him if it would be ok if I could get a pair of football boots. 'Bits?' Neilly said, 'You want a new pair of bits? New? New bits, son? You're only in the door two minutes.' I thought, 'Jeez, what's he talking about? This is the kit man, give us a pair of boots.' I remember the dressing room at Celtic Park, which I hadn't been in before, but there was this huge storage space at the back and Neilly went up and opened it and you could see all this stuff that was in there and I think he kept absolutely everything: strips, boots, gear. This was July '87 that I signed for Celtic and he gave me a brand new pair of Adidas World Cup '82 boots. They were brilliant boots and I used them in pre-season when we went to Sweden and played three or four games over there and the boots were fabulous. But I always remember Neilly saying that: 'You're in the door two minutes son and you want a new pair of bits? Ho, ho, ho, ho, ho. What have we got here?' That was Neilly and that was his style. He was great. They were the best days and I was playing with all my heroes, and Neilly was a great Celtic name. He loved the horses and was always in the other room waiting on the racing results."

Having encountered Neilly the joker, Walker would also quickly experience a softer more compassionate side to Mochan. This was a man who was able to gauge the mood of players and, if he thought it necessary, offer a quiet pick-me-up when confidence was low. Neilly had observed the master of man-management, Jock Stein, lifting individuals over a period of years as a player and manager and knew how to identify the idiosyncratic foibles of professional footballers. The power to tap into a player's sensitivities and drive their motivation was an underplayed facet of Neilly's character, as Walker elaborated. "We went over to Sweden and I was really keen to make an impression. We played a couple of amateur sides and I was struggling to make an impact. I think I played about three games and I hadn't scored but

I remember the first game because I didn't play well and I know it was the centenary year but we weren't wearing the centenary strips, we were wearing the older ones with the V-neck and Celtic crest. I think Neilly saw that I was a wee bit despondent, a wee bit too keen to try and impress, and he came up to me quietly afterwards and said to me, 'You can keep that jersey son. That's your first.' I gave that to my brother and it was a nice touch from Neilly but he tended to do some lovely things with various players. I mean, he wasn't always this great, gruff voice that you would hear. He would take the mickey out of everyone and laugh at some of your attempts at trying to score goals or win big games because he could always come back at you with fabulous tales of some of the teams that he played in and some of the goals that he scored.

"The backroom staff played a huge part in the centenary season success in my view because any time we went to play a big European game, a semi-final or a final, we went down to Seamill to prepare and you'd always have Neilly there. He'd always be sitting with Billy, Tommy Craig and Jimmy Steele, who was a fabulous guy to have around your squad of 15 or 16 players. Jimmy would bounce off everyone and his patter was magnificent. He would keep everyone at ease and he would chat up the youngest girls who were serving us our dinner and just have a laugh with them all, making us feel so comfortable. I loved those days going down to Seamill because you knew that if you were going down there then you were going to prepare for a big game. We always had these tremendous games on the grass just in front of the hotel and the losers went into the sea, which always made it really competitive. We tended to play the married men against the single men and I was one of the young ones who had just got married and that was great because I was in with players like Roy Aitken and Tommy Burns and we invariably won more than we lost. It was always a good laugh."

"We had big experience in players like Pat Bonner, Roy and Tommy, and I remember Neilly being around them in the changing room. He always tended to be doing something with their boots, changing their studs or whatever it was. When Billy did all of his work and addressed us as a group, Neilly would retreat into the back corner. Sometimes Billy would give Steelie a nudge and tell him to get up and give us a bit of his chat and he'd go through his spiel, and Neilly would be quietly going around doing his own thing. He wasn't one for a making any sort of grand speech, he was always quiet in the corner and it was a real contrast from when you approached him in front of people and he had this sort of gruff manner. He would always slap you down but with a bit of humour in it. These guys were a huge part of what was a really successful season and we all knew the type of legacy that guys like Billy McNeill had with his European Cup winning exploits and Neilly with the Coronation Cup win and beating Rangers 7-1 and scoring all those goals with that left foot of his. He didn't mention it all that often but once or twice when he brought it up, you knew where you stood."

The first meeting of the season between Celtic and Rangers resulted in a 1-0 victory for Billy McNeill's new-look Celtic side. Recent recruit Billy Stark scored a low drive after just four minutes and was on the receiving end of a vicious second half tackle from Graeme Souness, which resulted in the Rangers player-manager receiving his third red card since arriving in Scotland from Sampdoria. Strong words were exchanged in the tight Celtic Park tunnel after the game and it was none other than Neilly who stepped in to halt the querulous and moustachioed aggressor as he made efforts to get at Billy McNeill. Mochan had emerged from the battles of Montevideo and Madrid unscathed, so an early-season verbal onslaught at Parkhead would have left him completely unperturbed. He was clearly a man of many roles, and was even forced to re-emerge with his treatment bag for a later match.

"One of the funniest moments with Neilly was when we were playing at Tannadice," remembered Peter Grant. "Brian Scott had got an operation on his knee and couldn't come on, so Neilly came running on. One of the players had got injured and I was already squealing because I'd never seen Neilly coming onto the pitch before. Then I seen him going to spray whoever's on the ground and he's sprayed it and the spray's gone the other way and missed the player. He's then tapped him on the side of the leg and said, 'Right, you're alright son. Up you get and on you go.' I'm on the pitch at Tannadice thinking, 'I didn't just see that happening there.' That was Neilly for me. He was a fun guy and everybody loved him but he'd torment the life out of you."

Grant was a combative midfielder who had already spent seven years at Celtic Park and, at just 22, was from a generation of home-grown Celts who had grown up with Neilly Mochan's influence, antics and assistance in equal measure. Grant knew the importance of the centenary season to the Celtic supporters and appreciated just how pivotal Neilly's influence, however understated, was to this Celtic squad. "Neilly and Jimmy Steele used to work off each other fantastically well. They were two great characters. Having well-known Celtic personalities around the park was something that the club was always built on and I seen that in later years when John Clark took over. One thing that Neilly also had was that he knew a player. He was no dummy when it came to football and he knew how the game should be played. I think even though he was known as the kit man at that particular time, he was always there for the manager, who was able to lean on him. Neilly was very honest to the extent that he was cutting. If a player went in for a pair of boots in March or April and Neilly put them off, then that player thought that they were getting released or something. There was no chance that he would give out a new pair of boots so near the end of the season, knowing that they weren't going to be there next year. He was that type of character, he just always knew what was going on. I think he had more of an input than people were led to believe because of his football intelligence and understanding. Neilly didn't bother if you were the most senior player with a hundred caps or the youngest player in the squad. If he wanted to say something to you, whether it was positive or negative, he said it to you. The big thing that I learned from him was the professionalism. Ok, he was fun, but he didn't let anybody step out of line."

The glowing respect that Grant reserves for this legendary Celt is abundantly clear, and his memories of that dressing room, particularly during the club's centenary season, include plenty of classic Mochan moments. "It was hilarious watching Neilly in the dressing room. I know that he liked a whisky before the game and then he'd push his hair back with Vaseline. He used to have the football socks on every day. He'd have a suit on with a pair of football socks with tie ups. All he was missing was a pair of shin pads. Tracksuit trousers and a pair of football socks every single day. I can't think of Neilly as anything other than hilarious. He was outlandish really. He was way before his time in the way he went about in a dressing room but he was what football was all about for me. That is the sort of thing that people miss now.

"I used to sing the song to him, 'When the ball hits the net at the speed of a jet, that's a-Mochan,' and all that sort of stuff. I'd ask him to explain his Coronation Cup goal again and Neilly would come in and draw it on the board and say, 'I hit it from there son. I put it about there.' He told us it was from about the halfway line at first but then it got further and further back and he was in his own half by the time I left Celtic. He was some character."

Celtic's early season form was inconsistent and this prompted Billy McNeill to harangue his board for the purchase of a top-class strike partner for Andy Walker. Paul McStay's creative midfield displays were often rendered impotent by a lack of goalscoring prowess and, by the end of September, Celtic had been knocked out of the League Cup by Aberdeen and failed to progress beyond Borussia Dortmund in the first round of the UEFA Cup. Celtic supporters historically loved their heroes to have a personality to complement their ability, with Mochan's maverick team-mate Charlie Tully having been a cult figure in the 1950s. The rapscallion tendencies of Jimmy Johnstone endeared wee Jinky to fans and players alike in the '60s and '70s, regardless of his misdemeanours. Then 'Champagne Charlie' Nicholas became the pinup boy of the early '80s before his big-money transfer to Arsenal. Of course, the devilment must be balanced with talent for the relationship to last, and one player who undoubtedly fitted the terrace hero mould was Frank McAvennie. Flamboyant off the park and a phenomenal striker on it, McAvennie had become a star of English football with West Ham United after making a name for himself at Saint Mirren. When Celtic paid £750,000 for the Scotland cap on 2nd October 1987, it was a club record fee and McAvennie recalled going straight into the Celtic side the following day. "My first game was against Hibs and the gaffer told me to hold back in the changing room. Neilly held me back and all the boys went out. I thought the supporters wanted Charlie Nicholas, so I didn't want to run out on my own and get booed. As I was running out, wee Jimmy Johnstone appeared and gave me a cuddle and said, 'Just go out and enjoy yourself wee man.' Wee man? He was about five feet tall. I thought that probably summed up Celtic for me, and Neilly was part of that. He was part of that whole Lisbon Lions era. The Lions are hanging over Celtic, every one of them. They're all there, even the ones that have gone, God rest them, and that era will never be beaten. It will always be with Celtic and that's what makes it the club it is.

"Being a Celtic supporter, it was superb to sign for them. It was a big family club and there was a lot of tradition. Bobby Lennox was there with big Billy and Neilly. A lot of people thought that Neilly was quiet but he was superb. Every footballer likes a wind-up and Neilly was no exception to that. He liked winding all the young boys up and they would bite easier than the senior pros did. Neilly used to call football boots, 'bits.' I don't know if that's what they call them in Falkirk but the young boys used to go and ask, 'Mr Mochan, can I get a pair of boots?' Neilly would reply, 'Some bits? We never had bits when we won that big trophy with the big ears.' That's what he used to say to the young boys but they were all totally in awe of him. He would send them for a run and then he used to put tape on their boots and tell the boys they would last another couple of weeks. That was the make-up of Neilly Mochan."

McAvennie's debut ended in a lacklustre 1-1 draw, with Andy Walker heading passed Hibs' Alan Rough to score his tenth goal in 15 games. Andy Watson equalised ten minutes from the end and Celtic's new recruit looked impressive, if a little short of match fitness, in his first appearance. It took just a week before McAvennie scored his first goal in a Celtic jersey as Morton were beaten 3-1 at Celtic Park, and confidence began to grow in the Parkhead dressing room. "Just being alongside some of that Lions mob, Bobby Lennox, Neilly and the gaffer was brilliant," McAvennie explained. "There were others, like wee Jimmy Johnstone, who were coming in and out at that time and most of the boys would be in awe of them, especially Celtic supporters like myself. Neilly was there in the background and he just went about his business. I always found him great when I needed to talk to someone. He was good away from the rest of the boys despite being the biggest wind-up merchant in front of people. You could talk to him one-to-one."

It wouldn't take long before McAvennie desperately needed that kind of invaluable support. After just 16 minutes of his first Glasgow derby at Ibrox three weeks into his Celtic career, Frank was ambushed by Rangers' three England internationalists: Chris Woods, Graham Roberts and Terry Butcher. The Celtic striker ended up on the deck and, later, in the dock as he was ordered off along with Woods, and later Butcher, before all four players were reported to the Procurator Fiscal for breaching the peace. Fearing a public backlash, McAvennie found himself taken under Mochan's wing. "Neilly was brilliant. A couple of times he gave me a wee bit of comfort and solace. When I got sent off at Ibrox, Neilly was there. It was as if he just put a big arm around me and it was good to know that he was there. Neilly was good for that situation because he was unlike everyone else, who were coming in and shouting and bawling at me. I didn't realise that he was going to be there for me but he was. To be fair, Billy and the rest of them were all there after the initial reaction. I hadn't done anything wrong but neither did the Rangers boys and we didn't deserve to get sent off, never mind dragged over the coals in court. It didn't warrant that and it was nothing you don't see up and down parks every Saturday. There was disbelief that it came to that, and me and Neilly used to laugh because he thought I was delighted that it went to court so I got a week off training."

Frank McAvennie could have done with a wingman that sun-drenched afternoon at Ibrox as he battled three burly Englishmen, and it wasn't long before Billy McNeill brought one in. Joe Miller had spent the mid-to-late '70s being taken by his father – Joe Miller Snr, a professional footballer with Hamilton Academical and Swindon Town - to Celtic Park, where they watched the likes of Kenny Dalglish and Danny McGrain flourish. Joe Jnr's focus soon centred on his own game, and he was picked up by Alex Ferguson's Aberdeen at just 12 years of age. Boys' club football prevented Joe from seeing as much action as he was used to at Celtic Park but he regularly took advantage of the free half-time gate after his own match on a Saturday.

Joe had played under Jimmy Johnstone for Celtic Boys' Club at under-15 level and was approached by Billy McNeill after a Scottish Schoolboys' international against Wales in the early '80s. Although Celtic were bringing through players of the calibre of Paul McStay and Charlie Nicholas, Miller and his father decided that he should sign for Aberdeen. The Pittodrie side also had a decent track record for bleeding their own young players into the first team, and Joe was in the Aberdeen starting line-up by the age of just 16. On 13th November 1987, Billy McNeill finally signed the player that he believed would be the final piece of his centenary jigsaw going into the second half of the season. The player, for his part, fulfilled a lifetime's ambition. "I was only 19 when I signed for Celtic and it was a record fee for a Scottish teenager at that time," he reflected. "Barcelona, Atalanta and Sampdoria had all shown an interest and the day I signed for Celtic I received four telegrams from teams trying to sign me. Kenny Dalglish at Liverpool, Alex Ferguson at Manchester United and Terry Venables at Spurs, as well as Sampdoria, all wanted to buy me, but I signed for Celtic. I was an East End boy and I used to play football in the Calton and the Gallowgate."

Miller's debut arrived the day after he signed, as Celtic destroyed Dundee 5-0 at Celtic Park. The new Bhoy got on the scoresheet alongside Walker and McAvennie, who netted two apiece. Joe remembered his introduction fondly. "I signed for Celtic as a centre-forward but I could play anywhere. Billy told me he wanted me out on the right against Dundee and I more or less demolished them that day. Billy was reminiscing about how wee Jimmy used to play and that's what cut my throat. I was never going to play through the middle while Andy Walker and Frank McAvennie were on fire and I was providing them with goals. I got a goal myself and we just kicked on from there and were terrorising teams up front. I was just running at everybody and for the first eight weeks after I joined the club there was nobody going to stop me. I was fearless and really enjoying playing out on the right."

Miller had enjoyed a close friendship at Aberdeen with Teddy Scott, who was a former player and tireless servant of the club. When Miller arrived at Celtic Park, he instantly realised the importance of Neilly Mochan to the team's success. As Joe recalled, "Neilly was the sort of guy who had legendary status because he spent all those years at the club. All he ever did was live for Celtic and he was a real personality. He was the same every day that you went in and he was never up nor down. He did everything for us and could get us anything we needed. He would make a practical joke about it but he would always get you whatever you wanted. I got a boot deal for myself with Umbro and at that time all the young players would need to go and buy their own boots. I got it tied in with the deal that I got 30 pairs of boots sent to Celtic so that Neilly could give them to the youths and reserves and he was over the moon with that. He couldn't do enough for me. One Saturday he came into the dressing room and handed me my boots and when I looked down he had given me two right boots. It was a match day and I asked him to change them for me and he took them away like he'd made a mistake. What did he return with? Two left boots. He just stood in the corner of the room watching me to see if I noticed. He was lightening the mood before a game and had a sense of humour about everything he did, and that really helped us. The thing with having guys like Neilly in place at a club is that they pass on their vast experience. Neilly knew what the club meant to the fans. He had been there long enough and had seen managers and players come and go. So really, people like Neilly Mochan are the backbone of the club. They are the unsung heroes and play a hugely important part in the background. The service Neilly gave was phenomenal and he could tell you all the stories of the players he played alongside and the ones he coached. He could get players into the Celtic mentality so that they could appreciate what the club is and what it means. He kept you right on what not to do. He put Celtic on a pedestal and made you realise just what you were representing."

As a player, Neilly Mochan was the Smiler. By the time he returned to Celtic in a training capacity the senior players called him Neilly. So, now that he was the elder statesman of Celtic Park, how did Miller and his centenary team-mates address Neilly Mochan? "We called him The Moch," remembered Joe. "We sang songs about him. The atmosphere in the dressing room was top drawer. Those players still keep in touch with each other to this day and there was a good togetherness on the park and an even stronger bond off the park. We all did everything together. We partied together whenever we had time off and we all celebrated together. We used to sing songs and the one we'd sing for Neilly was, 'When the ball hits the net at the speed of a jet, that's a-Mochan.' It was like a waltz. We all used to sing that about him and he would sit at the end of the table loving it. He was just a total character and everything that he tried to do was to please the players but there was always a joke involved and he kept everybody's spirits up."

Celtic moved into December 1987 having won five games on the bounce since the arrival of Joe Miller. Neilly's old stomping ground, Cappielow Park, was next up and Frank McAvennie produced a spectacular individual performance, scoring all four goals in a 4-0 victory. As well as his own personal achievements that day, Frank remembered the game for a typical Mochan moment, "I was playing against Morton and I scored the last goal with a couple of minutes to go. I had scored four and I was substituted. I was thinking, 'What's Billy taking me off for?' And the gaffer just pointed and looked at Neilly, and he's sitting on the bench laughing. Neilly came walking into the changing room and I just had to laugh. I knew exactly why he did it because Neilly had once scored five for Celtic and he came in and said, 'You'll never beat me son.' And he was right, I never beat him."

Tradition still dictated that Celtic's New Year fixture would be against Rangers, and Billy McNeill continued more club customs when preparing for such high-intensity encounters. As Joe Miller recalled, "We were all Celtic fans and the atmosphere on and off the park was phenomenal. Everybody was together. We used to go to Seamill before we played Rangers and Neilly would take us for walks along the beach. We would go to the chapel before and after games. If we were staying at Seamill we would go to the Friday or Saturday night Vigil Mass. There was a good bond with us and we made sure everybody was involved. That's how close we were, we could play practical jokes on each other. We were all Glasgow boys, or Scottish boys. The only foreigners in our team came from Ireland. They were all good lads and they really bought into the Celtic way. They were all Celtic-minded people. We used to love hearing about Lisbon because this was the club that your family had passed down for you to support. To get the opportunity to ask Billy McNeill what it was like to captain the Celtic side and be the first British club to win the European Cup was incredible. We'd sit there and be in awe of him. He was managing you and passing these experiences on. For anyone who had the club at heart, this was the biggest thing you could ever listen to."

McNeill's side had extended their unbeaten run to 13 games leading up to the 1st January 1988 fixture against their greatest rivals, and their fans sang, "Happy Birthday Dear Celtic," as Frank McAvennie scored another two goals to secure a 2-0 win. Paul McStay was at his exquisite best en route to becoming Scotland's player of the year. McStay at his dazzling peak was, as Miller recalled, a sight to behold. "You get a huge respect for somebody when you're playing against them and when Alex Ferguson was the manager at Aberdeen we used to speak about stopping McStay. Ferguson's respect for what McStay could do was clear. He spoke about how he could hurt you with his penetrating passes and his bursts from midfield and how he kept the game simple. The Aberdeen side had a huge respect for Paul but I didn't realise how good he was until I actually played alongside him. That was when I realised how much service he provided. If I found myself in a sticky situation, I could give the ball to McStay and he would get you out of it. He would spread balls all over the pitch and he made it look simple. It was all natural to him and it became expected of him. I remember there were several European clubs after Paul and he could quite easily have played abroad but I don't think he had any ambitions to do that. Paul was a home bird and his family were all Celtic people, so that bond kept him at Celtic. If he had gone down south he would have been an absolute star."

Between the New Year's Day win and their next encounter with Rangers on 20th March 1988, Celtic remained undefeated. Indeed, they had not been beaten since Miller signed four months previously. A 2-1 victory at Ibrox followed thanks to goals from McStay and Walker, and Celtic were on course for a league and Scottish Cup double. Despite a raft of important fixtures standing between Celtic and centenary glory, Miller remembered that tomfoolery was never far from the player's minds. "We arranged to get Macca (McAvennie) picked up by Captain George, who did the 'Eye in the

Sky' in a helicopter for Radio Clyde. 'The Eye in the Sky' did the traffic reports and we planned that they would pick Frank up and drop him off at training just in time to wind big Billy up. We got Neilly to put a kit together and dropped it off at the helicopter pad and I remember we had it all arranged for a Monday. We were all ready at Barrowfield and Macca hadn't turned up. We knew that he had been down in London that weekend and he wasn't on time. We had already been out on the pitch and big Roy was taking the warm-up when we seen this helicopter hovering above Barrowfield. We're all thinking, 'Here he comes.' We're all looking up while we're stretching and laughing and big Billy comes over shouting and bawling, 'Where's McAvennie?' The next minute Macca jumps out of this car at the back of the pitch. He had absolutely bottled it and never got in the helicopter. We were all looking up at the helicopter thinking that it was going to drop him off. That was the sort of things that we got up to, and Neilly was well in on it."

By the time that Celtic clinched the league championship against Dundee on 23rd April 1988, they had already qualified for a Scottish Cup final against Dundee United. The centenary double was within touching distance, and Miller spoke to Billy McNeill around about this time about the manager's hopes for the future. "I remember big Billy having a conversation with us down at Seamill before the Dundee United game," recalled Joe. "We were on the lawn talking about winning the double and he spoke about trying to improve the side for the European Cup the following season. He wanted to bring one or two new faces in to boost the squad and get us a right good run in Europe. He was speaking about matching the achievements of the Lisbon Lions. That was how ambitious he was and how highly he rated that team."

Before preparing for the following season, Celtic had to overcome Jim McLean's Dundee United at Hampden Park on 14th May 1988. This was a fairytale season for Celtic and for Frank McAvennie. With just 14 minutes left to play, United were a goal up through Kevin Gallacher, but a double substitution by Billy McNeill – introducing Mark McGhee and Billy Stark - reinvigorated Celtic in the final 20 minutes of this enthralling match. McAvennie equalised on 76 minutes and scored the winner in the final 60 seconds to clinch Celtic a centenary double. "To score the two goals was magnificent but it was a team effort," the striker recalled. "There was no way we were getting beaten by Dundee United. We scored so many goals in the last couple of minutes in that season and there was an awful lot of pressure on us to win it because the supporters wanted it so much for the centenary year. I'll never forget after the cup final, I was sitting with Tommy Burns having a laugh on the pitch and Tommy had the base of the Scottish Cup. Neilly came over and Tommy started crying and I'm saying, 'What's the matter with you?' He said, 'You've got no idea, Frank. We'll be remembered in a hundred years for this.' At that, Neilly just said, 'Aye ok son, give me the base of that cup.' Tommy's emotions went right over his head and he just took the base and walked away. It was just so Neilly."

Buckets of sand were then dispersed over the centre circle of Celtic Park and moustaches laid out in the home dressing room along with the kits for a unique and unusual team photo shoot near the end of Celtic's momentous centenary season. Mochan historically had his picture taken only with 'good teams' and he was happy to be included with this particular group as he supplied the Vaseline for Tommy Burns, Roy Aitken, Paul McStay and the rest of the Celtic centenary squad to grease their hair into a 19th century style.

The resulting image is striking, with each player adorning an 1888-style Celtic jersey - thick white cotton with an oversized green Celtic cross within a red oval shield on the right breast. Neilly stands in the middle row with a towel draped over one shoulder and an air of Victorian authority contradicted only by his 1980s Adidas Sambas.

The strip that this team sported was first used by Celtic's inaugural manager, Willie Maley, who was still in charge when Neilly was born in 1927. In the front row is Scotland's finest player, Paul McStay, whose great uncle Jimmy was the wartime manager of Celtic when Neilly's senior career began with Greenock Morton in 1944. The club's finest scorer of goals, Jimmy McGrory, was the boss when Neilly signed on as a player himself in 1953 and as an assistant trainer in 1964. Neilly had then gone on to serve during the subsequent managerial tenures of Jock Stein, Billy McNeill (twice) and Davie Hay, playing the roles of trainer and kit man since the golden era of the '60s and '70s.

Neilly returned to the club as assistant trainer the year before top goalscorer Andy Walker was born and knew Tommy Burns when he was a bright prospect on the ground staff – a boy he would send down London Road for fish suppers on Fridays. He had sat in the dugout and witnessed every first-team match ever played by Burns, Aitken and Bonner in Celtic jerseys and had watched them develop from boys into men, assisting them throughout the process in his own quiet, or not so quiet, way.

It has been proclaimed that Celtic is a football club like no other. That being the case, Neilly Mochan was a Celt like no other. Mochan was a man steeped in Celtic history and tradition and, by 1988, had become an irreplaceable figure at Celtic Park. Only he and Billy McNeill from that iconic image knew what it entailed to win Europe's highest accolade. McNeill had carried the big cup down the steps of the Estadio Nacional podium, and Neilly carried it down the steps of Celtic's aircraft and on to Scottish soil.

Neilly had seen the game change beyond all recognition throughout his 44-year career, but could he have envisaged the impending transformation of fortunes at Celtic Park? Only six more team groups would line up this way, with Neilly deciding whether or not he would join them. He would outlast the management team, the board and most of the players. But he would only enjoy one more victory with Celtic as the club entered one of the darkest eras of its illustrious history.

CHAPTER 14:

THE KING OF KIT MEN

"Can Rangers win nine league titles in a row? I fear that we can't stop them from doing ten, maybe even more." These were words that Neilly Mochan would not have uttered lightly, and certainly not in a public forum. But in a private moment during Celtic's late '80s and early '90s implosion and near-extinction, he disclosed his greatest fear to his youngest son, Neil Jnr. This proud football club had been monumentally mismanaged for decades and the centenary celebrations and double-winning campaign had only papered over some craterous cracks. These cavities were too deep to fill with passion alone as the board's season-on-season failure to suitably invest in the stadium, training facilities and playing personnel left them light years behind their dark foes from the south side.

As Celtic arrived at Ibrox on 27th August 1988 for the first derby of the 1988-89 season, they had already lost one of their opening two league games and faced a Rangers side bolstered by yet another England internationalist in Gary Stevens. Meanwhile, Billy McNeill had been able to add just two new faces to his reigning champions, and both were goalkeepers. Leicester City's Ian Andrews and the ageing Alan Rough arrived for Celtic's European Cup campaign; signings indicative of the board's lack of vision and ambition. It is almost certain that these two players were not what the manager had in mind when he had discussed his plans with Joe Miller while overlooking Seamill sands the previous season. The cataclysmic 5-1 defeat that followed in that

August Ibrox encounter was Celtic's worst result against Rangers in almost 30 years, and so began the club's almost fatal downward trajectory. After months of speculation, top goalscorer Frank McAvennie rejoined West Ham United for £1.25 million on 18th March 1989. This was a loss that could and should have been avoided, as the striker explained. "Neilly was one of the few people who were there for me when I was leaving. He knew that I was a Celtic supporter and that I didn't want to go. But I was owed money by the board and they were refusing to pay and it was wrong. I should never have left the club. When I joined Celtic the first time, I thought I was going to be there for my entire career. So when they never paid me what I was promised it was hard for me to take. While the gaffer was shouting and bawling, Neilly was there for me. He was good that way because he was one of those boys who had been there, seen it and done it and he could talk to you. I didn't go to see him, he came to me. Neilly was there and he was always there. He knew when to wind people up in the dressing room and when to sit down with them and talk. Neilly was more than just a kit-man. He was a lot more than that, especially to me."

Despite a largely poor season in which Celtic relinquished their league championship to Rangers and finished third, Billy McNeill was still able to guide his inconsistent side to the Scottish Cup final, where they stood between Graeme Souness' cornucopia of expensive stars and a domestic treble. As part of their preparations for this mammoth encounter, the Celtic squad were taken on a pre-match trip to Portugal, as Peter Grant recalled. "Most of the boys were going golfing to relax but a few of us didn't play golf so Brian Scott, Neilly, Derek Whyte, Stevie Fulton and I went for a walk along the beach.

We had been out the night before for a meal and a couple of drinks and we stopped to get a coffee. It had been quite dull that morning but at mid-day the sun came out in force and that led to me asking Neilly if he wanted a wee half because I knew he liked a nip now and again. So we sat ourselves down on the beach, with the bar not far away, and we all had a few drinks. The sun was shining so we got the baby oil out and we're splashing this oil on like something out of *Rab C Nesbitt*, a typical group of Scots guys on holiday. I passed Neilly the baby oil and said, 'Neilly, get that on you. It's good for you and will soften your skin in this heat.' So Neilly starts rubbing this oil all over his face. We sat there until four in the afternoon and got absolutely scalded with the sun, I mean roasted alive. We were leaving a few days later to play Rangers in the Scottish Cup final and my shoulders were covered in blisters. We got sun stroke in the scorching weather and Neilly ended up looking like something out of *The Singing Detective*. We were getting ready to leave and I was covered in blisters and Neilly couldn't get his trainers on. We were like a couple who had gone abroad for the first time. All the boys were killing themselves at us on the flight home. Neilly's face was bright red and I couldn't move and this was our build up to the cup final."

Joe Miller had been recalled to the Celtic forward line in the lead-up to the Rangers game, and had scored the winning goals in each of the previous two league fixtures against Hibernian and St Mirren. That earned him the responsibility of leading the line on a blisteringly hot afternoon at the national stadium on 20th May 1989. "I always seemed to do well against Rangers and had always wanted to play in an Old Firm final at Hampden," Miller recalled. "My ex-Aberdeen team mate Davie Robertson told me when he later joined Rangers that Graeme Souness and Wattie Smith used to gear their team-talk around stopping me. They felt that if they could stop me playing and prevent me from servicing the strikers then they had a chance. I remember that Rangers used to double up on me and big Billy and Tommy Craig made me aware of that in advance. A lot of fans never realised that if I got past one defender there was always another one there."

Only one Rangers defender, the aforementioned Stevens, stood between Miller and Rangers' goalkeeper Chris Woods when Peter Grant's through ball was intercepted by the head of Richard Gough and nodded on by Mark McGhee. Stevens, the £1.25 million right-back, was woefully short with a pass-back to his international team-mate and 'Super Joe' pounced on the error in a heartbeat to score what proved to be the winning goal four minutes before the interval. The image of Miller blowing kisses to the Rangers fans in celebration had to be appreciated, for it was the final glory Celtic would enjoy for six treacherous and dismal years.

As the rot set in, Miller witnessed the decimation of the centenary side he had been so proud to have been a part of. "We were struggling to get key signings in," he said. "I remember Paul McGrath was close to coming up and he would have made a difference. After the centenary year we lost Frank McAvennie and we seemed to stop dead after that. A lot of our team were coming to the end of their careers and were moving on. Within a few years we lost Roy Aitken, who had given enough service and felt that he needed a new challenge, Mark McGhee, Mick McCarthy, Tommy Burns and Billy Stark. These were all experienced players. I was only 21 when all the old heads started leaving the side. The only experience that was left in the dressing room was Paul McStay, big Packie Bonner and that was it. I felt that Paul had to carry a lot of the flack when Roy left because he was appointed as captain and I don't think he was as influential a player when he was given that added responsibility. I think Paul McStay was a much better performer without the armband. Celtic got the best out of him in that centenary year."

The class of '88 were to be the last great domestically assembled Celtic team and, as the face of Scottish football changed irrevocably, so too did the signing habits of this once-proud bastion of youth development. Having previously boasted a fertile youth policy envied the world over, Celtic began to sign players from destinations as far-flung as Warsaw. And so entered Polish internationalist Dariusz Dziekanowski in the pre-season of 1989-90. "The foreign players and boys from England started coming in," remembered Joe Miller. "We had to explain the importance of the Rangers game to them. They had heard of the rivalry but we had to tell them that there was no bigger game in the world than Celtic against Rangers. You have your Milan derby and Boca Juniors against River Plate in Argentina but this was beyond football. We tried to prepare them for the atmosphere and explained that you can't hear anyone on the park as it is so loud. These new guys couldn't believe the intensity of it.

"Dziekanowski signed and we christened him 'Jackie.' You could see straight away that he was a very skilled individual with the ball. He used to keep it up in the dressing room and he had a real bag of tricks. He was doing all these 'round-the-world' moves and we were all standing there watching him with Neilly Mochan. Neilly then said in his Falkirk accent, 'You're not bad, son. I hope you'll be able to do all that when you go out on the park.'

Then the Moch went away and came back in with a table-tennis ball. He got Jackie's attention and told him to keep his eye on the ball. Neilly then threw it up to the height of the ceiling and when it came back down, he caught it on his forehead. He started walking around the treatment table balancing this table-tennis ball on his brow and he shouted, 'Open the door, open the door,' and he waltzed out of the changing room with his arms stretched out, balancing this ball on his head. We were all cheering Neilly on and Jackie's face was a picture. He thought it was the greatest thing he had ever seen. Neilly came back into the dressing room and said, 'Jackie, follow that,' and he walked back out again. We were all doubled up with laughter and Jackie was saying in broken English, 'Unbelievable. The skill of that man. So skilful. Did he used to play?' Jackie had no idea who Neilly was, so we explained that he was a Celtic legend and that he was now 90 years old and Dziekanowski took all of this in because of Neilly's white hair. But what Neilly had done when he went out to get the table-tennis ball was caked his forehead in Vaseline and when the ball landed on his head, it stuck to the jelly. Jackie was trying to catch a table-tennis ball on his head for weeks after that."

As the faces and nationalities changed around the familiar setting of Celtic Park, the kit-man remained a constant fixture. The European Cup Winners' Cup endeavours lasted just one round as Partizan Belgrade went through on away goals after an emphatic 6-6 aggregate scoreline. Dziekanowski's four-goal display at Celtic Park on 27th September 1989 became his defining moment in the green-and-white hoops and Mochan reacted in typical fashion. "I told McNeill that Jackie's a cream donut. You've had the cream and now you're left with the donut." Neilly's analysis meant that Celtic had enjoyed the most enjoyable part of the Polish striker's talent and they would be left with the less-inspiring elements from then on. He was not far from the truth as the Pole could look extremely impressive on his game. Unfortunately for Celtic, those days were few and far between and his attraction to off-field vices was well publicised. As Dziekanowski was filling in his Player's Union application form and listing his previous clubs, Mochan tapped him on the shoulder to tell him he had missed one. "Who?" asked the bemused striker. "Victoria's," came Neilly's deadpan reply. The early promise of Celtic's £600,000 striker faded like the Glasgow side's chances of a trophy, and the beaten Scottish Cup finalists languished precariously in fifth place in the league, just four points above second-bottom St Mirren.

Billy McNeill was on borrowed time, having received no silverware return on the additional £1.75 million acquisitions of Mike Galloway, Paul Elliott, John Hewitt and Dariusz Wdowczyk. The manager realised that season 1990-91 was make-or-break for him in the Paradise hot seat, and it was at this stage that a favourite of Mochan's returned to Celtic Park in the form of Charlie Nicholas. The ex-Aberdeen forward was joined by Hibs' John Collins, the club's first £1 million signing, and Arsenal's Martin Hayes. "I think he brought in Charlie and John Collins because they were Celtic-minded," recalled Joe Miller. "Tommy Craig was key to bringing in Collins as he had been a big influence on him at Hibs. Before I signed in 1987, big Billy was interested in signing Charlie from Arsenal. He eventually went to Aberdeen with the money they got from Celtic after selling me."

"They went to Germany in the pre-season," remembered James Butler. "Big Billy was raving about Martin Hayes to Neilly. He said to him, 'Wait until you see this boy. He's got it all. He can strike it, pass it, head it.' So they were playing this friendly in an open arena and Neilly's watching Martin Hayes when he turned to Billy and said, 'Hey McNeill. You've signed the wrong player here. That's Hayes the cricketer you've bought, not Hayes the footballer.' Frank Hayes had been an English cricketer and that's the way Neilly let Billy know that the boy was no good. He knew a dud when he saw one. If he went to a game to look at a player, Neilly would take a piece of paper and put a line down the middle. On one side he would write, 'Can play,' and on the other he would write, 'Can't play'. He made it as simple as that and within five minutes he obviously thought Martin Hayes came into the second category."

A little nonsense is relished by the wisest men and Neilly's art of applying humour to the tensest of situations was appreciated by virtually everyone at Celtic Park. On very few occasions during a 40-year period, the hunted became the hunter, and Joe Miller remembered one such rare scenario during pre-season in Germany, "After one of the friendly games we went for a meal with our opponents in their social club. The tables were set and Neilly came over with Jimmy Steele to sit beside me. I was sitting down and they were standing just behind me when the two waitresses arrived with the sauces and put them down on the table. It was piping hot pepper sauce so I just put them either side of me where Neilly and Jimmy would be sitting and put two soup spoons beside the bowls and said to the two of them, 'The boys are taking ages so you may as well sit down and get started.' Neilly and Steelie thought this was their soup and so proceeded to sit down and start eating it." Peter Grant looked on in astonishment as he recalled, "God rest them, they started eating the pepper sauce thinking it was soup. It was like that scene from *Mrs Doubtfire* when you see the cream running down her face. The sweat was dripping off them. Wee Steelie's eating away and I'm thinking, 'Is Neilly on the wind-up?' But the two of them actually thought that it was soup." The architect of these capers, Miller continued, "After a few spoonfuls Neilly turned to me and said, 'Gee wiz son, that soup's got a fair kick to it. What do you think of that Steelie?' and Steelie replied, 'It's hot alright, it's going for my false teeth.' They were sweating buckets and I couldn't help but start laughing my head off. The waitresses came over and asked Neilly why they were eating the pepper sauce. He just looked over and conceded, 'You've done me like a kipper, Miller.' It was the only time I remember ever getting one over on Neilly."

One of Mochan's ground-staff boys, Stuart Balmer, had graduated to the first-team for this German tour and made three substitute appearances during the trip. To his eternal regret, his impressive form did not enable him to progress further at Celtic Park but it did win him a move to Charlton Athletic as Balmer remembered, "I travelled to Germany and thought I was about to break through, but Charlton came in for me and my opportunity to play even one game for the Hoops never materialised. Paul Elliott had played with Charlton previously, so I went and spoke to him and he offered me some great advice and I decided to go. This was a big season for me as I was in the last year of my contract but I was summoned to Billy McNeill's room over in Germany and was asked to speak to Charlton, which I did, and they paid £120,000 for me. Sheepishly, I went to see Neilly and told him I was leaving and asked him for a Celtic jersey, but he chased me and I was gutted. Later on I went for my last meal with the boys and I told them all I was leaving to sign for Charlton. Neilly brought me over a jersey and all the lads signed it for me. That's the kind of bloke Neilly Mochan was and that jersey has always been a prized possession of mine. It's framed and still hanging up on my wall."

Yet another dismal, trophyless season signalled the end for Billy McNeill at Celtic Park. Only John Collins of the new batch of signings had impressed in dispatches throughout this torrid term and the nearest that Celtic came to silverware was as beaten League Cup finalists to Rangers. After two years without success, and with the imminent departure of star player Paul Elliott to Chelsea, it was no great surprise when 'Cesar' was eventually sacked by a board who had for years been significantly outspent by their most bitter rivals. "Liam Brady came in and he had to try and rebuild the team," recalled Miller. "He started moving a lot of the boys on and signed Tony Cascarino, Gary Gillespie and Tony Mowbray for big money. That's when I became a little disillusioned myself with all the comings and goings and The Moch must have felt the same. He had witnessed so many players and so many changes and yet he's still there as the kit-man and he never changed one bit. During such transitional times, guys like Neilly Mochan are invaluable to clubs like Celtic. These are the figures who carry the history of the club into new eras. He had been there for such a long time and he could tell the new faces all about the Celtic way of doing things. He knew what it was like to work with Jock Stein and how it felt to beat Rangers 7-1."

"Neilly always called it his work," remembered James Butler. "He would never say that he was going into the park or into training, he always described it as getting ready to go into his work. We were at a family funeral and I think he had taken a few hours off to attend. Tongue-in-cheek, I told him he better head back to Celtic Park or he'd get his books and he said to me, 'James, there are a lot of people in there who will get their books before me, don't you worry about that.' And he was right. He always reckoned that Bertie Auld would have been a great manager for Celtic at one point but he loved Liam Brady as a person when he came in. Liam was a genuine lad and Neilly would have warmed to that. There was nothing flash about Brady. He spoke to everyone with respect and on an equal level."

Respectful Brady may have been, but his big-money signings proved to be expensive flops as Rangers went from strength-to-strength in their quest to emulate Celtic's nine-in-a-row achievement of a now-bygone age. Irish internationalist Cascarino was a record signing and took until October 1991 to score his first goal for the club. By the time he scored his second, Liam Brady's side had suffered Celtic's then worst ever European defeat as they were humiliated 5-1 by Swiss cracks Neuchatel Xamax. Deadpan, Mochan once asked the hapless Cascarino at training, "Can you make chips, son? Because you can't play football."

It was a testing time for everyone with Celtic's interests at heart and the legendary kit-man began to notice changes to his daily routine that were being affected by an interfering and incompetent board of directors. "Neilly could size people up," stated James Butler, "and he had no time for the board members. I went to a reserve game with him once and he told me to get a seat in the main stand while he did his business in the changing room. I had taken a seat reasonably close to where the board were sitting and Neilly came up and told me to move. He didn't even want to sit near them, never mind talk to them." Denis Mochan recalled how the board attempted to exert their influence even within the confines of his brother's small corner of the stadium, "Neilly kept a bottle of whisky and a bottle of rum in his boot-room and it was tradition that the opposing managers would often go in for a half after the game. He would send Brian Scott up to the lounge to pick the bottles up whenever they needed replenished and they started getting him to sign for them. The board were even keeping tabs on simple expenses like that and things were changing for the worse at Celtic Park."

One tradition that Neilly would not allow to change was his affinity with the ground-staff boys at Celtic. He had taken on the mantle of being their mentor upon returning to the club in 1964 and had accepted a procession of young talented players under his wing from George Connelly and Brian McLaughlin in the 1960s and '70s to Charlie Nicholas and Peter Grant in the eighties. The next prospect to make an impression on Mochan was a central defender from his hometown called Graeme Morrison. "When Brian Scott heard that I came from Falkirk, he told me to ask Neilly for a run in and out of the park," recalled Morrison. "So I went into the boot-room and asked Neilly for a lift and was met with his look. 'A lift? Who are you, son?' But he started taking me home every day and that's how I got to know Neilly. The first-team and reserve players used to pile as many jobs on you as they could but Neilly looked after us. As we were travelling in together, he would give me more than my share of tasks because he didn't want anyone thinking that I was his favourite. Even when I got a professional contract I used to wait on Neilly and give him a hand before we headed home. On one occasion the ground-staff were due in on Christmas day and Neilly announced to them all the day before, 'Don't worry about tomorrow lads, you're all off for Christmas and Graeme is coming in to do your work for you.' I had signed as a professional by that point and didn't need to be in but Neilly would do things like that to make sure your feet were kept firmly on the ground. But he worked in your favour as well. I remember I was going to leave Celtic for Leeds United because I wasn't happy with my contract and I told Neilly I was going in to get my boots. By the time I got there Neilly had sorted it all out and I got the contract I was looking for from Celtic. He never mentioned it and I probably didn't realise at the time but that was Neilly and he was able to resolve everything no problem. He was a massive influence on that club on a daily basis. A lot of fans would look at Neilly and maybe just see him as the kit-man but he was so well respected within the ground. I remember different managers asking him for his opinion and guidance. I'm not saying Neilly had any say on who was playing because managers pick their own teams but he had a huge influence behind the scenes."

Liam Brady's second term in charge again ended in abject failure. Despite having spent over £3 million in his debut season, the Irishman was backed further by the board, who sanctioned the acquisitions of Albanian Rudi Vata and record signing Stuart Slater, from West Ham United. Both unanimously failed to impress the Celtic support, including James Butler who recalled, "Celtic played a friendly at East Stirlingshire and Rudi Vata ran out the tunnel wearing gloves. Neilly said, 'Vata must be cold,' and then he shouted 'Rudi, do want some gloves son?' and Vata's looking over completely oblivious, pointing at his hands. Neilly had a lot of time for Stuart Slater though, who got digs in Falkirk and spent a lot of time with him. It was a pity that he didn't perform."

Familiar faces Chris Morris and Derek Whyte moved to Neilly's former club Middlesbrough and the stocky striker Andy Payton was brought in from Ayresome Park. Graeme Morrison recalled Mochan's initiation of the Burnley-born forward, "I was in the boot room when the argument happened. There had been a build up of Andy Payton saying he could outrun anybody and Neilly was obviously winding him up and said, 'Look son, *I* could outrun you.' Andy took the bait and replied, 'I'll race you for any money you want,' and I remember Neilly saying, 'You go one way around the pitch and I'll go the other way and the first back lifts the money.' I think it was for a hundred quid so Andy Payton went away to get his money and I said to Neilly, 'You can't win,' and he just gave me his look. He put his Samba's on and went straight out to the old ash pitch around Celtic Park. It was a really sunny day and the two of them lined up. Andy was ready to go and Neilly had his two fingers on the track like he was going to do a sprint. All the players were there and shouting, 'Neilly, Neilly,' and the two of them took off. Andy was bombing it around with his big arms going because he could run. He had gone right around the first corner and Neilly had gone forty yards the other way before he stopped, turned and came back to the line. He picked the money up and said, 'First back to the line gets the money,' and he went straight up the tunnel. Everybody was rolling about laughing but Andy Payton was still running around the park. He had got to the halfway line and still hadn't noticed. Then he reached the corner flag and everyone is waving to him on the way up the tunnel. He came in raging but his money was gone."

Sadly, behind the laughs, Neilly's beloved Celtic were a sinking ship. The disappointment of four trophyless seasons was compounded by Rangers winning their fifth championship in a row in Brady's second campaign of 1992-93.

"I fear that we can't stop them from doing ten, maybe even more."

The catastrophic months that followed came close to burying Celtic and wiping them out of existence. The thought of life without this unique football institution became a distinct possibility and Liam Brady eventually resigned in October 1993.

"He was some man, The Mochan," explained the unequivocal Frank Connor, whose job it was to steady this ship and navigate the Parkhead side through three matches until a permanent replacement was announced. "People often say to me about having an unbeaten record as Celtic's manager. It was not about me, it was about doing what had to be done for our club. Neilly was there with me and we knew exactly what we had to do. We went about our business with no fuss."

The hapless board of Glasgow's East End giant had looked out over Kerrydale Street from their ivory tower for decades as hordes of faithful Celtic supporters flocked en masse to worship their green-and-white-hooped heroes. But where once Europe's finest were slayed, a decrepit arena, barren of glory, now stood. The appointment of Lou Macari as Celtic's eighth manager was the final throw of the dice as the vultures began circling paradise.

"When I took over as manager for that short period," explained Macari,

"I tried to get back to the simple ways of Jock Stein. One of them was that we ran to Barrowfield every day. The players didn't want to know. It wasn't for them, as they couldn't be seen running through the East End streets of Glasgow, and I found that hard to take."

The Celtic support would have found Macari's player recruitment equally hard to take and James Butler remembered that, even in such critically bleak times, Neilly Mochan could find solace in a wind-up, "He was the master at it. Paddy Crerand sent up two trialists from the army and they were playing a bounce match at East Stirlingshire. All the local Celtic fans were at the game and when the big centre-half walked out, one of the boys asked Neilly who the new player was. Neilly looked around each shoulder and then whispered, 'Paul McGrath, keep quiet.' It was the trialist from the army called Justin Whittle but from a distance he might have passed as McGrath, until he got the ball."

One man's influence had woven a meandering thread through each and every major development and success enjoyed by Celtic Football Club since 1953. Neilly Mochan was steeped in the Parkhead side's finest traditions but had also suffered many difficulties and failures along the way. However, nothing could have prepared him for what was to transpire on that fateful spring evening of 4th March 1994. Events leading up to that pivotal day had brought this beacon of working-class pride to its knees and the club that had created so many heroes desperately needed one of its own. As the haunting cheyne-stoking cry of its final living moments echoed harrowingly around the East End of Glasgow, wilting garlands settled beneath falling rain outside this once-great Paradise. The appellation of 'saviour' was one uttered and prayed for by the assembled thousands whose strained expressions were etched to mourn their team's last breath. Fortunately, Fergus McCann arrived like a Croy Express via Canada and just seven minutes before the death-clock rattled its final chime. A £9.4 million investment saved the club from ruin and began its transformation into a first-class modern empire. When the dust settled on this miraculous takeover operation, McCann was challenged on his knowledge of the club's history by being asked to name his all-time favourite Celtic player. The shrewd and wily businessman nonchalantly answered without hesitation, "Neilly Mochan".

Following the ousting of the previous regime, Celtic naturally entered a period of immense transformation, for they had to, and Macari's days were numbered under McCann. His replacement would be welcomed with open arms by Parkhead's amiable kit-man, who had seen him develop from 'Wee Tam from the Calton' on the ground-staff at Celtic Park to the manager of this club in recovery. "Tommy Burns came in at a time when a new stadium had to be built and there had been demonstrations by the fans," explained Billy Stark, his friend and assistant manager. "He was a Celtic legend and knew exactly what was required in terms of bringing everybody together. Tommy and I had only been in management for a couple of years and so we were going back to a massive club at a fairly young age. We saw a huge job in front of us and we were looking for wee things to reassure us when we came back in. Neilly Mochan was very much one of those. He was his usual confident, unassuming self and settled us both down by giving off that aura that we knew so well."

CHAPTER 15:

A FAMILY MAN, A QUIET MAN, A FOOTBALL MAN

"When Neilly took ill, I can remember going into the house to visit him and he was lying down on the couch and that was something you never saw him doing," lamented nephew, James Butler. "Celtic were due to go on a pre-season tour and Neilly had a problem with his leg and I told him that he shouldn't be going anywhere. It was Tommy Burns' first trip as manager of the team and he didn't want to let him down; he wanted to help Burns get started. That is how much Celtic and Tommy meant to him."

"I think we were in Ireland for pre-season when I learned that Neilly had leukaemia," remembered Andy Walker. "He was in the dressing room picking up all these strips and the young boys were just sitting around not helping and I remember taking Paul McStay to one side and he gave the boys a bit of a rocket."

"I would often see Neilly when I was at the games," remembered Father Brian Gowans. "He would be sitting in the dugout and I sat just behind him in the main stand, so I used to give him a wee wave if he looked up." Father Gowans was the parish priest at Camelon and assistant at St Francis Xavier's in Falkirk. It was there that he got to know Neilly's sister, Nan, who was the housekeeper at the chapel, and a friendship with the Mochan family flourished. "When the news of his illness was broken," continued Father

Gowans, "it was Nan who told me and there was a sadness in the church. It really put a downer on things. We were all so sorry to hear of his diagnosis because, although he wasn't particularly old, we all realised that he was never going to recover from that. It was a question of time but he was a man of faith and he had great family support. I met with Neilly and administered the sacrament of the sick, which is a tradition in our church. There was that calm acceptance. He knew what was happening and he wasn't afraid. I suppose, being human, his thoughts went out to his family. When you are the father, the grandfather, and the breadwinner of a family, it is not so much where you're going to but what you're leaving behind. Neilly knew that he had a good, strong family who would look after and care for each other, so that was less of a worry in one sense. There was a benign, calm acceptance from Neilly, who realised that this was the next stage of his journey, and he faced it well."

"He knew what was wrong with him but he wouldn't tell you," recalled James Butler. "Then he went to the hospital and I went in to see him and he said to me, 'Well that's it James. The baw's burst.' And that was when he told me. I'd go up and sit with him and we'd talk about being in the Celtic changing room and all the great nights we had going to the dogs. It was terrible. He was brave as a lion though, brave as a lion."

"I went up to the hospital with my brother, Willie, to see him," said Denis Mochan. "He was getting agitated with the medication and then he said to us, 'For heaven's sake' - that was one of his great sayings - 'that Gemmell and Johnstone are up to their nonsense again.' He was lying in bed and I said to him, 'Well, you tell them. You're the gaffer.' And he said, 'Aye, you're right. I'll sort them out.' His mind was wandering a wee bit and it was such a shame."

"I was asked by Frank Connor to do the kit for Neilly because he wasn't well," reminisced Graeme Morrison. "Once the game was over we had to get in the bus and take all the players into the Falkirk Royal to visit Neilly and I was sitting outside because I had already been in to see him. I was really close to Neilly and he was shouting me back in. He was always winding me up and I wouldn't go back in and I told him I'd see him the following day. He kept saying, 'Come back', but I never went back in and it was that night that he passed away. Even though I knew he was ill, I always thought that it was Neilly and so he would be alright."

In the early hours of Sunday 28th August 1994, Celtic lost one of its greatest sons. Neil Mochan passed away quietly in Falkirk Royal Infirmary after a short but brave battle against leukaemia. Joining Celtic is akin to being adopted by a surrogate family and Mochan had proudly served this family as man and boy over five different decades. The head of the table was gone and the Celtic fraternity were thrown into a state of mourning by their loss. The man who had worked under seven managers at Celtic Park embodied the spirit of this unique club. He was a working-class hero in life and he became a Celtic icon in death.

As a player, 'Smiler' possessed the most ferocious shot in Scottish football. The strong and tenacious left-footer rejuvenated Jimmy McGrory's Celtic when he signed in 1953 and went on to immediately win the Coronation Cup before inspiring his side to a league and Scottish Cup double in 1954. His finest moment in the hoops undoubtedly came in the 1957 League Cup final when he scored two as Celtic destroyed Rangers 7-1. As a trainer, with a streak of silver appearing through his immaculately greased head of hair, 'Neilly' adorned his bottle green tracksuit while fine-tuning Jock Stein's men as they outplayed and outran anyone who dared enter the Lisbon Lions' den. The players he trained won a European Cup in 1967 and nine Scottish league titles on the trot, and his boot-room was the envy of clubs the world over. As a kit-man, 'The Moch' wore a white doctor's jacket to match his perfectly-groomed Vaseline-thick hair, and his all-seeing-eye oversaw the early '90s demise, and the beginning of a revival, of a loved and served so well.

"When you speak about coaches and friends," asserted Bertie Auld, "Neilly ranks highly in both those categories for me. I promise you, as a friend you couldn't ask for better. As a coach, he was one of the best although he was rarely given that title. When he was ill, never at any time did he ever mention it to us. He never changed throughout that time and he was a very strong person inwardly."

"When I got the news that Neilly had passed away," recalled Father Gowans, "I got into the car and drove down to his house. Mary was sitting in her chair in the corner of the living room and I went forward to her. I got down on my knees, took her hand and offered her some sympathy. I was quite fixed on Mary when I went into the house and I wasn't aware that the room was actually choc-a-block full of people. I looked around after a few minutes and there they all were. The first one I saw was Billy McNeill and then there was Jimmy Johnstone, all the Lisbon Lions were there. I don't know if my jaw dropped but it probably did because I suddenly went from seeing Mary to seeing all my boyhood heroes in the one room chatting away and sharing stories about Neilly's life.

"Being a family man is a huge connection which is not lost on Celtic. The club has that family feel and if you're a fan then you belong to that family. That is how it felt that day with the heads of the Celtic family all gathered in one room, and it was a terrific moment. Although it would have been a sad moment for Mary, she would have been proud as punch to have all of Neilly's friends in the room and talking so fondly of him.

"Our tradition is that the body is received into the church the night before the funeral, so we had a ceremony at St Francis Xavier's where we received Neilly's body into the church and a lot of the Celtic family were there. On the day itself, it was standing room only in the church and the service was relayed on speakers outside. Anybody who had anything to do with Celtic were there from the Lisbon Lions and the first-team to the boys' team. I noticed that Walter Smith and Archie Knox were in attendance as well and they were then the management team at Ibrox but would have also known Neilly from their time together at Dundee United. Billy McNeill did one of the readings and Tommy Burns did the bidding prayers. I was in heaven seeing them taking part in a mass I was celebrating, and it was a celebration of Neilly's life. Funerals need not be morbid and sad and this one certainly wasn't, although it is never easy to say farewell to someone.

"We focused on Neilly's time with us and I based my homily on three words all beginning with the letter F: Faith, Family and Football. Those three things meant a great deal to Neilly. He was a real man of faith and came to church regularly. He prayed a lot and thanked God for his family, whom he was very supportive and protective of. He was a terrific father and grandfather and his family felt very safe and secure with him around. And his appetite for football never left him. Neilly never really retired. Up to the day he died, if he could have done anything for Celtic then he would have done it. You would have to consider a combination of those three things to find the true spirit of Neilly Mochan. We then went to the graveside where there was a huge crowd and a mass of flowers, mainly in the Celtic colours."

"I went to the graveside and the man upstairs looked after Neilly that day," recalled Bertie Auld. "What a beautiful sight it was. I couldn't believe he was gone. When you are younger, you go to christenings and engagements and then you normally attend marriages and 50th birthdays. Then once you get to a certain age, you are visiting people in hospital and you suddenly realise that it all goes in so quickly.

"Whenever Mike Jackson, Paddy Crerand and I get together we always look back and speak about Neilly, even to this day. Although he is not here, he is always in our thoughts. Neilly played such a big part in our careers but he wasn't one for pushing himself to the forefront. After Lisbon they couldn't find a brown paper bag big enough to cover my head but Neilly remained completely down to earth."

"I think it is absolutely crucial to have people like Neilly at a big club," stated Davie Provan. "That is why so many foreign managers who come into the English game will keep someone who has an affinity with the club. Jose Mourinho kept Stevie Clarke for years and Louis van Gaal has Ryan Giggs. It is very important that you have someone who the supporters recognise and can relate to as well. Celtic is a very emotional club and there are maybe only two or three like that in the whole of Britain. Liverpool and Newcastle are the others and they are driven by emotion. The supporters like to see some of the old players around the ground and still being involved with the team. It is part of the identity of the club.

"If you got to know Neilly well enough, then you could call him Smiler. I was at the club maybe seven or eight years before I could call him that because you had to earn the right. He had played the game at a good enough level to know what was going on in your head and you very rarely got a compliment from him. You would get one when you weren't playing well and were having a hard time. Maybe when your confidence was low, that's when you would get one from him and if you got a compliment from Neilly it was like a lottery win because they were few and far between. I remember being up at the park after I had left Celtic and I was working for Radio Clyde. Neilly poked his head out the boot-room and shouted, 'Provo, come here,' and I went into his boot-room. He opened the whiskey bottle and gave me a wee nip and I thought, 'That'll do me.' For Neilly Mochan to pour me a half, he must have had a respect for me. Wee things like that meant so much, yet you really had to earn it with Neilly because he was old-school and he had this veneer of hardness and coldness about him but he was anything but that. That was just a front."

"Celtic is a tradition and, although they keep saying it, it *is* more than just a football club," asserted Frank McAvennie. "No matter what happens, they will always be a massive part of my life. I think the players who weren't fans of the club when I was there certainly became Celtic supporters. People like Neilly, Jimmy Johnstone and Bobby Lennox were all around the club and it was great to have them there. They were like part of the furniture and it was brilliant for a supporter like me to see all these guys in and around the place. All the boys from the Lisbon Lions era are immortalised and Neilly Mochan is up there with the best of them."

"I think that it's vitally important to have people like Neilly Mochan around Celtic Football Club," stated Bobby Lennox. "Modern players come in and don't know much about the club but if you have a guy like Neilly about then he's a constant reminder of Celtic's history. Neilly was great for our team and great for the club."

"Neilly probably served under more managers than anyone else at Celtic and that speaks for itself," surmised Graeme Morrison. "Any successful club has got to have their cornerstones. Managers will come and go and having someone in the background like Neilly is invaluable."

"I was brought up with both of my grandfathers running Celtic supporters' buses, so I knew what the club was about," explained Peter Grant. "But Neil had actually played for Celtic and every day I would look at him as someone who had lived it. He gave me an idea of what it would take to be a Celtic player. It was only when I moved to England that I realised why so many people struggle to play for a club like this. It often wouldn't be anything to do with them being a bad, good, or indifferent player. It was just about being able to handle that your job is to represent the club 24 hours a day, seven days a week and every day of your life.

"I've been to clubs since I left Glasgow at 32 but people will always describe me as Peter Grant of Celtic and it is with great pride that I accept that. I know a big part of that was down to Neil Mochan and the people I grew up with at Celtic Park. They made me so proud of the fact that I had an opportunity to play there. It was only through those great people, both on and off the field, that I was given that opportunity. Those days on the ground-staff are so special to me. I will never forget them and I still use some of the banter that Neilly used with me when I was 15, and I'm 50 now.

"The small details that I take with me to this day came from Neilly. I tell players and I tell my son to make sure all their kit is inside out once they are finished with it, that everything is folded, that everything is put back the way it should be, that your laces are open in your boots, that you never leave your kit for anybody else to tidy up. That all came from Neilly Mochan because he told me to do that every single day on the ground-staff at Celtic Park. And whether it was Danny McGrain, who was a senior player during my time, or Tommy Burns, God rest him, they all had to do the same. Neilly treated every one of us the same and every one of those men had such great respect for him. Unforgettable times and an unforgettable person.

"We still tell stories about Neilly to this day and we have such a high regard for him as a person. He was some man and very much part of every memory that I cherish from my time at Celtic. When you leave this earth, you only hope that people will always remember you with fond memories and it is great to be able to say that I knew Neilly Mochan.

"When you aren't involved in the football environment, it's the dressing room and people like Neil that you miss so much. Him and Jimmy Steele made your day special and these were the things that you looked forward to every day. At the time, they were as important to Celtic as any player was. The family of Neilly Mochan should be very proud that he will be remembered for evermore at Celtic Football Club."

"Neilly was a huge loss because he was the oil in the machine," reminisced Father Gowans. "He never left that club and he'd be there to give support and guidance to the new players coming in. More than just preparing things for them, he had a wealth of experience and knowledge and knew the game back to front and he knew the pitfalls. He was called 'Smiler' for good reason because he would make people laugh and he was always smiling himself. When Neilly went, Celtic lost more than just a former player. He made a fantastic contribution to that family and he's up there with the greats as someone who should never be forgotten."

"I miss going to the ballroom dancing with my man," was the poignant reflection of Mrs Mochan. "We danced all over. I used to go to Glasgow when Neil played with Celtic but I wasn't too interested in going to the games. We went to quite a few places abroad over the years and I remember going on the trip to Portugal. We brought up a good family, two sons and four daughters, and when I say my prayers I let Neil know how his family are doing. Every night I say 'goodnight' to him and every morning I say 'good morning.' He's still with me."

Neilly Mochan made an instant impact at Celtic Park upon commencing his love affair with the club in the early '50s. The Celtic support admired the man as much for his indomitable spirit as for the talents he displayed on the field of play. His cherished unorthodoxies were reserved mainly for his colleagues as he fulfilled the roles of player, trainer, assistant masseur, sponge-man, guardian of the ground-staff and, finally, kit-man during a career that left an indelible impression on the deeply illustrious chronicles of

Celtic Football Club. The sight of those splendorous green-and-white hoops remained inspirational to the man who hailed from Carron. The jerseys he attained became collectable, fetishised masterpieces. From the classic 1950s, 60s and 70s designs - functionally minimalist yet invitingly sublime - to the striking and often wacky abstractions of the 1990s. Bequeathed to his youngest son of the same name, the museum-worthy collection is as vast as it is eye-wateringly unique. Mochan had an unbreachable affinity with this club with which he will eternally be identified and he possessed a loyalty that is sorely absent in the modern game. In the 21 years since Neilly's passing there have been numerous abhorrently technocratic changes to the game he so adored. But, as the cost of watching football continues to price out many working-class families, the life's blood of this national pastime are becoming increasingly aware of the need to return to some of the innocent traditions of the past. The memory and value of valiantly genuine ambassadors of clubs like Celtic continue to be celebrated as they percolate into the modern fan's consciousness.

Tributaries to Celtic's most-celebrated figures were erected around the facia of their world-famous stadium in 2015 and the iconic images are redolent of the Glasgow club's proud history and traditions. The legacy of Neilly Mochan lives on as he features twice on this impressive visual installation that adorns the pantheon of greats where lions sleep and legends are made. Neilly smiles down on his widow, Mary; on his family in Scotland and extended family in Australia; on brother Denis and sons Neil and John, who are still Celtic season ticket holders; on his grandchildren and great-grandchildren; on the Denny Celtic

Supporter's Club that bears his name; and on each and every one of us as we walk up The Celtic Way to paradise.

"When I went to Paradise, I looked down on Neilly sitting in his seat. Now that Neilly's in Paradise, he's in his seat looking down on the rest of us." - Father Brian Gowans

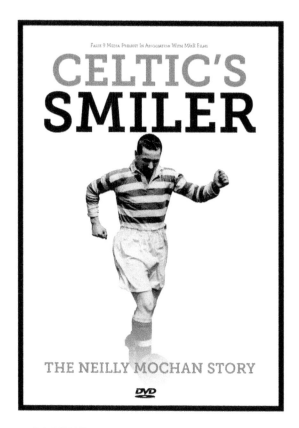

Lightning Source UK Ltd.
Milton Keynes UK
UKOW05n0334241215

265276UK00009BA/112/P

9 781473 328150